HOW TO COLLECT
THE "NEW" ANTIQUES

HOW TO COLLECT
THE "NEW" ANTIQUES:

What They Are, How to Evaluate Them

By ANN KILBORN COLE

DAVID McKAY COMPANY, INC.
New York

HOW TO COLLECT THE "NEW" ANTIQUES

Library of Congress Catalog Card Number: 66-14586

MANUFACTURED IN THE UNITED STATES OF AMERICA

VAN REES PRESS • NEW YORK

To all my friends in the antique business who have held my hand through the maze of turn-of-the-century relics and pointed the way to markets and prices

FOREWORD

LIKE most authors and authorities on antiques, I have not, until recently, been willing to go beyond the Victorian era in researching my four books and my articles on antiques, particularly those that appear weekly in the Sunday magazine of *The Philadelphia Inquirer.* Until a few years ago I felt that the year 1900 wrote *finis* to any discussion of really worthwhile old things, and that it would be some time before we could begin to define a new period again. But things move fast these days. I was soon faced with a surging interest on the part of my readers, and the antiques-conscious public generally, in a whole new era of antiques—that of 1890 to 1925. Consequently, I have spent a good part of the past few years finding out everything I could about these newcomers: which items are valuable as antiques, and what they are worth in dollars; their claims to quality and long life; when and where they were made; where you can most readily find them, and so forth. The research has been just as fascinating as digging in the kitchen middens—the old household dumps—for the relics of earlier times.

But an experienced author digs in strange areas. And so it has been possible for me, with much work and insatiable curiosity, to put this book together from many sources: From my own memory—oh, dear, yes!—and the recollections of several reliable older friends whose span of remembrance goes back sixty years or more; from talking to those who have learned their New Antiques lore from handling the items discussed in the various chapters—this includes dealers, auctioneers, and even the dedicated buyers of these new-old antiques; from observation in antiques shops and antiques shows, where sometimes I felt like a spy who was still out in the cold; from auctions where I went to listen, not to buy; from encyclopedias; from examining old wholesale and mail-order catalogs; and from the several antiques magazines, *Spinning Wheel, The Antiques Journal* and *Hobbies,* especially. The handsome *Antiques* yielded little because, happily for many of us, it still holds the line to the 18th- and 19th-century finds in the antiques world. Occasional articles and reader letters in these magazines have answered my own questions and filled in the gaps. From their advertisements I have been given an overall look at prices and markets across the country. My thanks to them all and to the few individual writers who have dug into the small unexplored corners of the antiques world in these turn-of-the-century years.

ANN KILBORN COLE

TABLE OF CONTENTS

TABLE OF CONTENTS

HOW TO COLLECT
THE "NEW" ANTIQUES

CHAPTER 1

WHAT ARE THE NEW ANTIQUES?

I THINK it important to find a name for this period, roughly 1890 to 1925, when people were making and using what today are often called "the new antiques." Some people have used this term to describe Victorian relics, but Victorian antiques are no longer new. They are still very popular, but they have been around now for some years. Some are using the phrase *turn-of-the-century*. It is very descriptive, and you are beginning to hear it on every hand. It certainly sets the period.

In 1901, the long reign of Queen Victoria, covering a span of almost seventy years, came to an end. In fact, what we call the Victorian era in the history of antiques really ended earlier, about 1890. This post-Victorian era, from 1890 on, is, according to the authorities who have given it thought, the third period of antiques in this country, the first running up to 1830 and called *The Age of Craftsmanship;* the second from 1830 to 1890, the period of *Mechanization* and accelerated commercial production; and the third from 1890 to ... when? What will the books call this third period and how many years will it cover when the story is told? It is reasonable at this point in time to establish its end as just after World War I, when a whole new set of standards and tastes took over and we began to produce what we call *Modern*.

This thirty-odd years was a period of slow change. Life in this country at the turn of the century still retained some of the characteristics of the Victorian period, sentimentality, somberness, a sense of propriety and decorum, and even some of the Victorian bad taste. Nevertheless, there were omens of a trend to less formal living. As we passed the century mark, a restlessness began to be felt, and the United States, along with much of the world, no longer felt secure and isolated in a pool of well-being.

I am old enough to remember how my own girlhood was still tempered by Victorian standards. No matter how strongly a new sense of daring might have prompted me to speak to strange boys on the merry-go-round at Atlantic City, I never yielded to the impulse. No nice girl spoke to strange boys without being introduced. I can remember meeting the mother of a dashing young architect from Dublin and having her remark how glad she was to have him interested in me because I was "such a nice, safe, girl." Inwardly I seethed, but outwardly I kept to the proper demeanor expected of me. Incidentally, I had my first drink in public with him and felt like Susan B. Anthony waving the banner of liberation for my sex while I sipped. I can also remember the furore that pulsed through the dining room at college the night a daring senior came to dinner flaunting lipstick.

When I went looking for a newspaper job after college I

was told paternally by one editor after another, "Why do you want to get into this work? It's no place for a nice girl. It hardens a woman." Parenthetically, I did manage to get involved in the fourth estate, and if I became hardened I was not aware of it, only blissfully full of a sense of liberation. I was a novelty, a newspaperwoman, not a nurse or a teacher like most of my more circumspect classmates.

In England, the accession of Edward VII to the throne sparked a general loosening up in all fields. It was a happy time in which to be alive, no wars, no taxes, no disturbing ideologies. As the rebellion against Victorian conformity grew, more thought began to be given to convenience, comfort, space, and freedom. This was a time of elegance for the moneyed classes. The English photographer, Cecil Beaton, has often recreated this feeling in his settings for pictures. The delightful costumes and sets of *My Fair Lady* epitomize this elegance.

It was an anomalous time, in fact an anonymous time, with not enough character to give it a name if we do not adopt the English term, Edwardian, which accounts only for the first ten years of the century. But things in America were happening fast. In a very short span of years, scarcely a generation, we saw the opening of two big links with the rest of the world, the Atlantic Cable and the Panama Canal. The horse car gave way to the mechanized trolley car and the subway, the automobile arrived, and the telephone came into use in many private homes. The first years of the century saw the home use of electricity, central heating, and indoor plumbing, at least in the cities.

By 1910, we were enjoying the phonograph, the nickelodeon, the carpet sweeper—and silk stockings. In these years, except for the depression of 1907, there was money to spend and new things to spend it on. The rich grew richer and didn't care who knew it. They displayed their wealth in tremendous houses and lavish entertainment. A single ball could cost over $300,000. One social leader, Harry Lehr, gave a sumptuous dinner party for his dog, and Mrs. William K. Vanderbilt gave a dinner for a monkey.

With increase in foreign travel, interest in things from abroad increased, too. Many pieces were brought back from Europe to replace cumbersome Victorian furnishings in the new palatial residences. Furniture, china, glass, silver, armor, bronzes, and tapestries from many parts of Europe, especially France and Italy, made museums of houses large enough to absorb them. Sometimes whole rooms from English manor houses were set up in American millionaires' homes. Statuary from Italian villas furnished the grounds. There were palaces such as Viscaya, the Deering showplace in Miami, Florida, built in 1916. The various Vanderbilt mansions—Biltmore, in Asheville, North Carolina; Hyde Park; Beaulieu, and the Breakers, in Newport, Rhode Island—still stand as monuments to the lavish life the rich enjoyed during the early days of the century.

Nothing like this flood of *objets d'art* and furnishings from abroad had ever before been such an important element in establishing American taste and values. Sometimes the display was almost vulgar. One heard for the first time the expression, *nouveau riche*. Today, many of these palatial homes have been given away to institutions for charitable or educational purposes. As these "Newport cottages" and similar mansions all over the country have been cleaned out, the galleries and antiques shops have become crammed with the relics of this gaudy past.

In the middle classes, change was not so abrupt during this

time. In lieu of fine American furniture, families had to be satisfied with the Victorian pieces made to outlast one or two generations. A few learned to cherish family pieces handed down from earlier periods, and another few, the vanguard of the antiques-minded army swelling with recruits today, began to buy up the discards of earlier years at what we now consider bargain prices. But even in the middle brackets of income, imports, often given as wedding presents, began to fill the shelves and cupboards. It is these items, among others of the late 19th- and early 20th-century origin, that are being sought after and sold in the antiques shops today.

Things accelerated after the depression of 1907. Until 1915 there was a turbulent period of industrialization, with a flood of new things to tempt the courageous buyer. World War I put a stop to much new manufacture, but during the war, and immediately afterward, America broke completely with tradition. Young girls drifted to the offices and manufacturing plants to take the places of the men. Many women at home were forced to do more of their own work. Social barriers began to break down. College girls—what few there were—began to talk about careers, and, like myself, began exploring fields beyond teaching and social work. Quantity rather than quality, unfortunately, was the prize concern of the manufacturer and builder in all lines. Houses were "jerry built" and goods were "ersatz."

Until 1925, we as a country had not accepted the period called Modern in our overall taste, although the *avant garde* here was bringing back good examples of it from Europe. These years, 1890 to 1925, were a time of transition.

Many items that attract today's collectors give us clues to the way of life in these transition years. We still valued some kind of formality and propriety. We had not learned to be truly casual in our home life or in our clothes. Men still wore a variety of hats, and many—not just the politicians—possessed top hats, which were kept in leather hat boxes that you can find in antiques shops today. For business, a man chose a derby. Tails were the proper dress for formal occasions; the tuxedo was tolerated only for stag affairs. A man carried as many gim-cracks on his watch chain as a woman used to carry on a chate-laine hung from her belt. His beard went, but his mustache remained. He used a straight razor, which he sharpened on a strop—very handy when Junior had to be chastised. Perhaps he kept his personal shaving mug at his barber's, very likely one with his name on it in gold, or with a picture of his trade or profession transfer-printed on it in color. For some time he continued to wear "longies," even after steam heat came in. He also still wore "boiled" shirts with stiff bosoms and sepa-rate collars and cuffs, some made of rubber or celluloid.

In cleaning out the attic of my old home I found my father's collar box made of some kind of pressed-paper composition—very pretty now on my desk for paper clips and such. It brought back the memory of days when all the laundry was done at home and when the battles with the washboard, starch, and bluing made Monday a day to be dreaded and endured. For, you see, my father was a professional man, a doctor, and there-fore had to start each day with clean linen, at least with fresh white collar and cuffs. No relaxed, button-down collars for him, or any other white-collar man in those days. A man in that period carried a cane and was not ashamed to wear a flower in his buttonhole, even to the office. He wore spats with his low shoes. Golf called for plus-fours and auto trips for dusters and goggles. He was emerging slowly from the customs of Victorian years but not so fast as his wife.

By 1900 the silhouette of the woman of fashion had entirely

changed. The bustle was gone. Balloon sleeves were in; the hour-glass figure of the Gibson Girl was the vogue. Shirtwaists, one of the first concessions to the new informality, were adopted with perhaps a high boned collar and jabot to keep the neck covered. The leg was still a limb, but ankles began to show. Petticoats began to dwindle in number until only one was left, and that likely a silk one that rustled effectively. Bicycling was popular for women who often wore divided skirts *"pour le sport."* Schoolgirls wore bloomers and middy blouses for gym classes and that exciting new game of basketball. The flannel or mohair bathing dress of the 90's was out, but the female figure was still well-covered on the beach with stockings and beach shoes for good measure.

For the auto, a woman wore a linen duster and a veil tied down over her hat as protection against the wind and the dust of the road—there were only 144 miles of paved roads in the country in 1900. She never drove a car until the self-starter came in, but she could handle a fashionable electric brougham by moving a single handle. As my delighted mother exclaimed when we acquired an electric car, "Why, I can handle it with my white gloves on!" It was a ladies' car, with fancy glass cornucopia vases for fresh flowers, a luxury for deluxe cars. We kept ours in the old stable back of our city house where my father's faithful old horse, Dolly, and his buggy waited ready for sick calls night and day. The stable also housed a monster, a huge generator that supposedly charged the electric cells of the car. At such times the stable glowed in a blue light and the smell was freshened with ozone. But the generating machine broke down so often that finally the car, the flowers, and my mother's white driving gloves disappeared, as did so many of such innovations in those days.

The sheath gown arrived from Paris in 1908, a daring step

forward in style. It was followed by the slit skirt and the hobble skirt that limited locomotion to shuffling, six-inch steps. Short skirts did not reach the knees until the Roaring Twenties. Formal dresses still had trains. Bonnets had given way to hats with brims that grew larger as pompadours grew higher. Girls wore their hair in "puffs" under their beaver hats, which were trimmed with ostrich plumes. There was always a veil caught under the chin and over the hat brim to keep the hair tidy and give a bit of glamor. Fans were still evident at evening affairs, usually of ostrich plumes, lace, or spangled chiffon. (Collectors never overlook these.) Pattern companies were encouraging women to make their own clothes, a threat to the family dressmaker and to the ready-mades that were beginning to fill the shops in regular women's sizes and even in stylish stouts.

Home entertainment in those days was mild in character, with guessing games, lotto, parchesi, and Old Maid to pass the evening hours. Most of these games can be found in antiques shops today. A party was dressed up with much crepe paper, place cards, and favors. Hostesses vied with each other in working out parties with unusual themes. I hate to think of how a fellow writer, Nellie Ryder Gates, and I contributed to these sometimes bizarre productions with the ideas we offered in the articles we sold to the women's magazines. We got more fun out of planning such things as a "Calorie Caper," an "Alphabet Jamboree," a "Hobo Picnic," or an "April Foolish Frolic" than did the poor, exhausted hostesses who tried them out. We would sit convulsed by laughter at the things we dreamed up and carried to such ridiculous lengths. I know the readers loved them and I'm sure they really gave such parties, but I know I never gave nor attended one. My battered thesaurus opens naturally to the page under *Amusement*,

Number 840, where words such as *romp, gala, fete, revels, junket,* and *antic,* spurred our imaginations.

A few courageous card players forsook hearts and whist for bridge; some of you may remember the ritual "I bridge it" from those early days. There was a piano in every parlor and group singing around it. Music companies did a good business with sheet music of the popular songs that are collected avidly by buyers today. Remember "Mary Is a Grand Old Name," "Japanese Sandman," "I Love You Truly," and "Under the Bamboo Tree," and many more catchy enough to be revived today by modern combos? Sherry was served instead of cocktails. Even small dinner parties followed a more or less formal menu: oysters on the half shell served on special oyster plates, a hearty soup, fish, fowl or roast, and a molded ice cream. It took some time for the salad course to take hold. Spinach, in spite of Popeye the Sailorman, had a hard fight getting included in an over-starchy family menu. My mother used to call it, "the broom of the stomach," but that didn't help it go down any easier. Except for the Heinz famous 57 varieties, most pickles and jellies were made at home. Until World War I, there was often a maid in the kitchen who doubled in brass, or rather aprons, a capacious one for cooking and a white one for serving in the dining room. She was summoned by a table bell or an electric button under the foot of the hostess. The tea table with its spirit burner and brass kettle still had its place in the parlor, ready for afternoon callers.

Conversation in the early years of the century shuttled from the fight for woman's suffrage (won in 1920); laws regulating child labor (not finally defined until 1941); Carry Nation (1846–1911) and her violent fight for temperance; simplified spelling; the flood of immigrants (the quota was not established until 1921); and Alice Roosevelt's wedding in the White

House to Nicholas Longworth in 1906. People went to the theater to see Maude Adams in *Peter Pan* in 1905, the Flora-dora Sextette and the Ziegfeld Follies, a novelty in showman-ship, in 1907. At the opera they applauded Caruso in *Pagliacci,* Mary Garden's acting (about 1907), and Geraldine Farrar in *Carmen,* only a few of the greats whose voices were crystallized on Red Seal records. I get a great satisfaction in confessing that "I heard them when," which happened because of an arrange-ment I had with a young art student in Philadelphia who shared her student tickets with me. They cost only $1.00 and admitted us to any unclaimed seat in the Academy after 8:00 P.M. Opera tickets then as now were a luxury, especially for young people.

Well-worn books on the library shelf were those of Edith Wharton, especially her tragic *Ethan Frome* (1911); Richard Harding Davis, the dashing Ian Fleming of his day, whose *Ransom's Folly* appeared in 1902; Finley Peter Dunne's Mr. Dooley stories, and, beloved of the ladies, Temple Bailey, whose books appeared as regularly as the seasons. On the silent screen (the full-length talkies did not come in until 1928) Mary Pickford, Douglas Fairbanks, and Charlie Chaplin delighted audiences in the new movie palaces in the second decade of the 1900's. Movie-goers roared at the antics of Mack Sennett's bathing beauties and sighed over the daring sex symbol, Rudolf Valentino, in *The Sheik*. The *Castle Walk* introduced a new style of dancing, as well as the boyish figure and cropped hair displayed by Irene Castle.

In one generation newspaper headlines recorded the discov-ery of radium (1898), the assassination of President McKinley (1901), the discovery of the North Pole by Admiral Peary (1909), the reaching of the South Pole by Colonel Amundsen (1911), the sinking of the *Titanic* (1912), the killing of the

Russian royal family and the establishment of the Bolshevik state (1918), the formation of the League of Nations (1919), and the attempted coup in Munich in 1923 that resulted in the imprisonment of a man named Adolf Hitler.

Yes, there was plenty to talk about in those years before Mao Tse-tung, Khrushchev, and Castro were even heard of. This is the world from which our new antiques come. Many are still in use in homes, unrecognized as antiques, and discarded ones that fill the shops are being gathered up by forward-looking dealers. Ten years ago they would have been found only in the junk or second-hand stores in which the white elephants and trash were dumped at house-cleaning time. Today, you are lucky to find "sleepers" or bargains even in junk piles or at rummage sales. These sources have been well combed by antiques hunters. In fact, it is not going too far to say that there are no bargains in antiques today, early or late. Everyone is too well-informed, sellers and buyers alike. The junk shop, in many instances, has moved up in the social scale of merchandising and often announces "Antiques" on its sign. Many dealers are honest enough to qualify their wares, when they are turn-of-the-century, or later "antiques," with such names as "This and That," "Bygones," "Then and Now," "Yesterday's Treasures," "Grandmother's Attic," "Antiques and Junque," or "Etc., Inc." One dealer, refusing to use the word antiques, calls her things "refined junk." But the shops do not always apologize for their stock. They feel, and perhaps rightly, that their wares are candidates for the title of antiques, which status they are on their way to achieving.

This brings up the much-argued question of age. "How old must a thing be to be an antique?" It is the first thing I am asked when I am introduced or recognized as an expert on antiques. In the mind of the average person, one hundred years of age seems to make an article antique. If it belonged to a grandmother or a great-grandmother, then it must be antique, no matter what it is. I try to tell such questioners that age is not all that matters in establishing a piece as an antique, that, in fact, it is often not so important as other things, particularly quality. I point out that there are many things made from 1890 on into the first quarter of the century that have all the makings of antiques—except perhaps great age.

Presumably, in defining antiques, there must be some attention to age, present or potential. Many recently made pieces are called "antiques of the future" because their quality prophesies a long life. But, everything considered, the older a thing is, the better. In foreign countries, where history is a matter of many centuries, you can expect to find antiques hoary with age. But in America we have not so many years to call on, hardly three hundred years. Nor did we have the population in our early years to produce many workmen skilled in the making of what we now call antiques. But even in England and on the continent the antiques are giving out, and dealers abroad are now being forced, as we are, to bring out more recent treasures to meet the overwhelming demand both for home use and for export. In fact, it is said that British dealers are coming to the United States to buy antiques, many of which originally were brought over from England when our own country was young.

One date puts a punctuation mark on the age of antiques in this country: 1830. This is the year set by the government to divide antiques, which are allowed duty-free entry, from taxable imports. This date was chosen because it was thought to be the end of hand-craftsmanship (regarded by many as a requisite in an antique) and the beginning of the machine age. Whether it will ever be changed is questionable. One of our most outstanding museums, Winterthur, near Wilmington,

Delaware, embraces only the years 1640 to 1840 for its exhibits of Americana. But while customs men and some dealers still stick to this limitation of 1830, most antiques shops do not. Too many of America's best treasures were made or imported after 1830, such outstanding items as Gaudy Dutch and Tucker china, Hitchcock chairs, Sandwich glass, and Bennington pottery. One dealer with years of experience and a national reputation behind her still asserts that she will handle only early Americana and nothing made by machine, but she is unique. The quality shops that carry only pre-1830 pieces make up a small percentage of the thousands of antiques businesses scattered throughout the country. And so we are forced to say that the age of antiques has widened its point of view to include, first, the Victorian, and now the things made or used in the first quarter of the 1900's.

Even if pieces seventy-five or fifty years old don't always deserve to be considered antiques, they are attracting the buyers. The shops could not do business without them. Many of the older, established shops that prefer to handle only the fine old stuff or primitives, spurning the recent imports, have been forced to fill in with later items. Let's face it; we are living in the middle of an antiques-hunting explosion, with interest in old things so great that there are not enough pre-1830 antiques to go around. More people know more about antiques and where to go to find out about them. I am continually being blamed for aiding this extension of knowledge, and, I suppose, considering all those who tell me that they have read all my books and consult them regularly or that they paste my weekly articles in a scrapbook, I can't be held blameless for contributing to this increase of knowledge and the consequent inroads on the market. But I can't feel sorry about it. If we are bound to have more buyers of antiques I prefer to see them informed, even if the market suffers. I am convinced that the more people know the better will be the things they buy; good things will not be passed by in favor of trash.

The supply of old things would seem to increase when collections are broken up and put on sale, but the market does not always gain by such sales because the desirable pieces often go back into cold storage and are kept there by new collectors. Neither do the old houses yield as much for the market as they once did. There are not as many old houses to be cleaned out. It is said that in desperation some dealers watch the obituaries so they can be the first to approach the heirs with offers to buy. All good dealers know the old houses and what they contain within a wide radius of their business. They wait patiently for the time when these antiques will come on the market. But even this does not always work, for people today, even young people, tend to hold onto the pieces they have inherited because they know their value. Or they may offer them for such ridiculous prices that no dealer can afford to buy them and hope to sell at a profit. And so it is no wonder that a new dealer venturing into the antiques business will find himself stocked almost wholly with items dating from no earlier than 1890 or 1900, things that have no great value and have not until recently been considered antiques.

One good thing about these new antiques is that they are fairly available; they have not been around long enough to have been entirely bought up. Moreover, they were mass produced and put out in quantity; a buyer does not have too much trouble finding what he wants. It is easier to pick up a piece of Limoges china than one of early spatter. In comparison with older things of a similar nature, they are less expensive. Those who cannot afford to pay $125 for an 1838 Gaudy Dutch cup and saucer, or $75 for a marked Danforth pewter basin of about 1810 can console themselves with a late Dresden plate of about 1900 for $10 or $12, or a pewter confectioner's mold may be only forty years old for $8. There is in my cupboard a glazed green pottery bowl shaped like a cabbage head that looks like majolica—but it isn't. I get as much pleasure from it as I would from a fine Whieldon piece costing thirty or forty times as much. My mother bought this almost fifty years ago for $1. She always used it for her delicious cole slaw.

The mass of antiques buyers today no longer come from the high-income brackets. Those whom the bug has bitten can find antiques to fit their pocketbooks if they are not too demanding about what they buy. Unfortunately, too many shoppers for antiques do not care what they buy at all, just as long as it is old and like what everyone else is buying. It is the day of fads. Hot numbers, as the dealers call them, will fill the shops for weeks or months; the prices will rise, and then suddenly interest lags, and the impulse buyers go on to something else. For a time it was iron sewing-machine bases for turning into tables; then calendar plates; then coffee grinders or decoys to be turned into lamps. Now it is Victorian "candlestands" (which are not candlestands, really, but small stands made to hold plants or statuary busts in the Victorian parlor); deacon's benches, small versions of the long antique settees, which are usually cut-down pieces or reproductions; and R. S. Prussia red-mark china, imported from Germany in the 1890's. There are more buyers today but also less discrimination and information in their buying.

Sometimes buying is motivated by nostalgia. These new antiques are so young that many of us can remember them used in our own homes. "Why, my mother had a blue pitcher exactly like that when I was little. She used it for lemonade. I wonder what became of it," a buyer will murmur wistfully.

Then she will pay $10 or $12 for a spongeware pitcher of common pottery because it brings back memories of peaceful summer afternoons on the back porch when there were no income taxes or a Soviet threat to bother one.

The decorators have a lot to do with this interest in things of the early 1900's. Their trained eyes detect the possibilities in these items and their imagination and ingenuity can work the most impossible relic into an interesting conversation piece for a modern room. Sometimes I think they seek these pieces simply for the shock value. A gaudily decorated chamber pot becomes a planter, a bowl from a washstand set will be used as a punchbowl, a wooden salt box will hold the roll of paper in the bathroom, a row of small plaster busts act as hat stands in the coatroom. People like to be shown how to make use of such outdated items in an amusing way.

A word currently going around in art and antique circles—"camp"—applies to many of these new antiques I have been talking about. Its meaning is a bit vague but it indicates anything "way out," bizarre, even outrageous, with amusing or ridiculous overtones, which was in its time considered seriously. In Eric Partridge's *Dictionary of Slang and Uncommon English* he defines it as meaning "something pleasantly ostentatious." Any overtone of another unpleasant meaning does not hold in this new use of the word. Pop art is camp, so are the garish Tiffany-type dome lights of leaded glass. Things that were once boring or banal are adopted as conversation pieces or for fun collections. Sometimes this is the only reason why certain articles of the period, 1890–1925, are carried in the antiques shops. Some shops have made the most out of things like comic books, stereopticon slides, mustache cups, bisque piano babies, auto radiator caps, Billiken figures, and the like.

Fortunately for the status of antiques generally, and for the future of the businesses that sell them, not all sales are based on whimsy, nostalgia, fashion, or price. Quality and lastingness among the newer things are there for the discriminating buyer to discover. Many good things, in china and glass particularly, made from 1890 to 1925 were logical steps in the development of American skills and ingenuity even when they were commercially produced. Many imported pieces are valuable because they build up the picture of the American way of life over the years surrounding World War I. Whether American or imported, they deserve to be saved from the trash barrel. When the fads die out and the fashions in collecting shift, the good things will stay and eventually take their places in the gallery of true antiques.

In this book I want to point the way to what is good in this transition period between the Victorian years and the beginning of the modern age. I hope it will give the reader the information that will help him avoid the pitfalls and take advantage of the good things before they become too rare and impossible to find. I hope it will help him to pick and choose from the mass of the johnny-come-lately antiques, to differentiate the trash from what will someday become treasures.

CHAPTER 2

EVALUATION

HOW is one to evaluate the antiques of this period from 1890 to the end of World War I? How can the average person sift the good things from the bad and decide what is worth buying for keeps? Unfortunately, there is not a great deal of help available. As yet little has been written about the collectibles used and made in the first quarter of this century, although material covering some of the classifications is beginning to appear on the market, inspired, no doubt, as is this book, by the questions of an interested buying public. Even magazines in the antiques field are more apt to cover the important collectibles of earlier years rather than items made more recently.

The reluctance of experts to give much importance to recent collectibles is partially due to the fact that they don't consider them true antiques. Also, since reliable information about them is hard to come by, it requires a lot of digging, mainly in catalogs and advertisements, to determine the truth about values, makers, dates and places when items were made, and other pertinent information. As a matter of fact, the dealers who handle these late items probably know as much about them as anyone else, since information passes among them, and in this way, bit by bit, the backgrounds of newly discovered pieces are established. Not so long ago very few dealers knew what Weller pottery was; today it can be found in all its varieties in the majority of shops. Dealers look for marks, learn what they mean, then compare unmarked pieces with those that are marked and identify them in this way. Specialists in any one line, such as cut glass, can reel off the names of makers without hesitation. They seem to pick their information out of the air. It always puzzles me how so many can know so much without leaning on a large library of reference books. But there is no doubt that handling pieces of a certain kind, seeing them, feeling them, weighing them have great advantages over merely reading about them in a book or looking at pictures. And so, one of your first steps, if you are or are about to become an amateur collector of late antiques, is to find a good dealer who really knows what he is selling, and take his word for it.

In establishing the value of new antiques the same criteria are used as those you apply in judging older pieces—is it in good taste, and what is its quality? I'd hate to be put on a panel with experts and asked to define good taste. It is a personal thing, and I believe you are lucky to be born with it or to acquire it through education or environment. It is a recognition of certain standards accepted by the era in which you live. Thus the tastes of one generation are not those of another. We no longer sip tea from a saucer but a hundred and twenty-five years ago it was done by the most cultured people.

When we go against our instinctive tastes in selecting something made fifty or more years ago, we often do so for other reasons, perhaps for nostalgia, or because a piece is amusing or historically important, as I have pointed out. One cannot dogmatically declare that everything old should have a claim to beauty. What beauty is there in an old t lunchbox or an old nursing bottle? But there are some standards a good antique should have. It should not be shoddy, pretend to be what it is not, or show awkward lines or bad form where it could have been graceful; where it was intended for use, it should have been practical. Of course, if beauty of color, form, or design can be added, so much the better.

For example let's set up a row of antique plates: an 18th-century blue Canton porcelain; a Gaudy ironstone of 1850, with Imari patterning; a late Dresden porcelain, with a dainty embellishment of flowers; and a modern plate, with free-form treatment of lines and daring colors. They are as different as chalk and cheese, as the English say, yet good taste will accept all of them. Good taste could also accept a Royal Bayreuth rose tapestry plate of 1900, while rejecting a silly little red devil-and-card pitcher from the same factory and date as merely amusing. Or you might prefer a piece of Haviland china with delicate forget-me-not decoration from the turn of the century to a garishly decorated slipware plate of the early 1800's, but you cannot deny that both were created with an effort at taste on the part of the artist in relation to his time.

Quality is more easily defined. It has to do with the way a piece is made, with material, manner and technique of decoration, line, form, finish, glaze, etc. A piece might have been conceived in perfectly good taste but turn out to be lacking in quality. Take period styles in furniture. There were good and bad pieces in everything, Queen Anne to Empire. A squatty

Queen Anne chair with an awkward splat and squat cabriole legs does not have the quality associated with the best of that period. Or the wood of a Chippendale-style chest might not be of the best type of mahogany, or the proportions could be bad even when the wood is good and the carving fine. It takes a practiced eye to spot such things. A book like Albert Sack's *Fine Points of Early American Furniture* with comparative photos of good, better, and best brings out this point very clearly.

The quality in a fine piece of Sèvres porcelain, or in American Tucker china, is easily recognized, but that does not mean that the sturdier ironstone of the same period does not have a quality of its own. It was made primarily for service, and there is integrity in its simplicity, honesty, and satisfactory function, with no false pretensions about being other than what it was. We have to look for quality in various ways.

That is why we can say with honesty that many of the antiques put out from 1890 on have real quality, though modern tastes might find it hard to accept them. Quality makes the difference, for instance, between a beautiful piece of Tiffany iridescent glass and the pressed Carnival glass that was a cheap substitute for it. The quality in Carnival glass, if judged by the prices asked for it today, should be considerable, but it isn't there. It was never there. The iridescence is superficial, it is gaudy in coloring, the glass is heavy, and the patterns are no better than those in any late pressed glass. Many people call it ugly and shudder when they see it, but many others like it and buy it because it is available and on the bestseller list at the moment. In spite of its popularity, however, it is doubtful that it has enough quality to carry it very far along over the years. I know I am going to hear guns popping at me from all directions because of this statement, but this is the way that I, and a lot of other people, feel.

The value of a piece depends also upon what you are buying it for. Generally, there are two kinds of buyers for all antiques. One expects to use his piece either by incorporating it into the furnishings of his home or displaying it there as a conversation piece. Then there is the collector, who doesn't buy mainly for use, but in an effort to accumulate as much as he can in a particular area, usually everything pertaining to one kind of thing, salt cellars, banks, molds, and so on. Or he may narrow down to one division of his subject, beginning with, let's say, French china in general, then going to Sèvres or to French flowerpots. Many of the items made in the early 1900's are still usable today and are an enhancement to a room when properly placed. But considerably more of these objects are the concern of the collector who is looking for variety and number in his area of interest. Many of the things to be mentioned in this book will fall in this latter class, and so their quality is not so important as is availability for collecting, particularly to the beginning collector.

Some collectibles will offer amusement and spur conversation. Some will reflect an old custom, some will illustrate a departure from the pattern, some will just fill in the picture of the thing collected as it existed fifty years ago. If you are after tin nutmeg boxes you may find ten or twelve different kinds, none of which are used today. Maybe you want powder boxes for the bureau. You can look for them in hand-painted Limoges china, cut glass, silver, opaque glass, cranberry, satin glass, wavecrest art glass, Nippon (Japanese), or Bayreuth (German), or silver deposit. Some will be good, some not so good, but the quality will not be half so important as the variety they offer.

It is usually the experience of the collector that at first he buys everything, but as the collection grows he becomes more knowledgeable and discriminating. If your collection is just a passing hobby and you can afford to indulge in it, it does not matter too much how good are the things you pick up. What matters to you is the search and the triumph when you find the elusive or odd thing in your category. But for those things that you are going to use or display in your home, look for the best. It pays. Buy less, but buy better, is always a good maxim for this kind of collector to keep in mind, whether it is for the trivial or the important. There is a financial consideration, too. When it comes to selling at some future date, as either you or your heirs may have to do, the good things will not only retain but undoubtedly increase their value in dollars and cents over the years.

What about the prices for these late antiques? In comparison with many older pieces, some of them are quite reasonable. There are areas, however, where the age does not seem to have anything to do with the price. Neither has rarity, because, so far, most of the later items have not disappeared from the scene, though some things are getting harder to find. But popularity does affect the price drastically. What everyone wants is sure to rise in price, often far beyond its real worth. A small animal-shaped pitcher of German china, which might have been a cheap novelty in variety stores a few years ago, can now cost well over five dollars. I am amused when I look at a little pink glass paperweight on my desk, an owl perched on a stack of books. Several times I have seen others like it displayed among antiques in the shops. But mine was a present from my son when he was only six. He had ten cents to spend at the five-and-dime store and the little pink owl caught his fancy. It has been my talisman for many years, but intrinsically, as an antique, it is really worth no more than he paid for it. It has always been this way. Except in some categories, the original price was usually far below what is being asked today for the new antiques. Look over the catalogs—and get a laugh. At the turn of the century a Coin Dot water set of pitcher and six tumblers in opal glass could have been bought for one dollar. Today it would cost $30 or more. A Mary Gregory vase that originally sold for fifty cents would bring $50 today.

It is no wonder that you hear sighing and crying about the high prices on every side, from the dealers as well as the buyers. I'm afraid that there is not much to be done about it short of a depression in the economy, and this is not foreseeable in the near future. As long as there is enough money around to be spent on luxuries—and to most of us, antiques are a luxury —prices will continue to be high. They are in tune with the times when everything else shows a rising graph.

There are many reasons for the rise in antiques prices, some evident, some not so evident. First we must remember that an antique is a "one-time" thing, especially if handcrafted. Even the production of commercially made pieces was limited to a few years. This makes for rarity to a degree. I have spoken of the demand that depletes the supply and raises prices. I have also explained how many former sources of antiques are drying up. Those who have antiques to sell are keeping the prices up for collectors and dealers. But while some collectors are cagey, preferring not to buy unless they can get bargains, others will pay anything for something they really want. The dealer buys to make a profit—if he can. But his margin of profit is shrinking unless he can mark up what he buys to even higher prices. While most other businesses have a usual markup of 40 percent, today an antiques dealer is lucky if he gets 20 to 25 percent on the average, less if he has a big turnover.

Another thing that swells prices is the dealers' habit of buying from other dealers. This sounds foolish, but it is often necessary. Every dealer has his specialty and his customers who want certain things. So he shops to get them, perhaps from another retail dealer or from a "picker," a middleman who covers a lot of territory and knows where and how to find antiques to pass on to the dealers who don't have the time to do this kind of searching any more. Or he buys from a wholesaler of antiques with tremendous stocks fed by many sources. In each case a certain profit over the original cost is involved. Almost every shop now allows what is called a "dealer's discount" varying from 10 to 25 percent. This gives the purchasing dealer a base for adding on his own profit, which may come to more than the first asking price. But this discount cuts into the profit of the dealer who gives it unless he in turn has marked up his prices to take care of his dealer clientele—which often happens. And so the private buyer is caught in this price adjustment when he buys retail. Every time a piece passes from one dealer to another it goes up in price. Some dealers will not sell at a discount to anyone. They keep their original prices firm for everyone—a much healthier thing for the antiques business.

For the retail buyer there isn't much advantage in shopping around; prices seem to meet a certain level. Price guides play a large part in this uniformity. As in every other kind of business, the older, better-known firms can get higher prices. A big dealer can afford to wait to sell a high-priced article. Sometimes a small dealer will take what he can get—if he needs cash. But overall, the prices average out and remain generally high. There are no bargins any more. Sometimes shoppers think they can get the price down when they discover a crack or a nick, a dent or a rough spot. But the dealers usually price such pieces to reflect the imperfection and mark them "as is." Small cracks and chips are not so important as they used to be because of the scarcity of proof pieces. One dealer of reputation says philosophically, "I always pay the price asked for a really good thing no matter how high it seems because I know that someday I will not be able to get it at all."

Here I'd like to explain the prices I quote in this book. They are approximate, intended only to give the reader a broad idea of what he can expect to pay in any certain instance and at this time. Prices vary from dealer to dealer in spite of price guides and in various parts of the country. They can change overnight because of some sudden demand or publicity. That is why I cross my fingers in using the dollar mark when I discuss the things currently sold in the shops. Even by the time this book is published, a piece could have risen drastically in price, or possibly—but not too likely—dropped. Experts have computed that in this rising antiques market, you can expect an average 10 percent price increase a year.

Will present prices hold up? Some will and some will not. Often there comes a stage when prices stabilize because dealers realize that they can price an item right out of the market. The public will go just so far, though often the price limit seems very slow in coming. When popularity and demand die down, prices may slip off for certain things, but how far they will go depends again upon quality and also on availability. Fads come and go. Often a fad demand dies down simply because people get tired of an item, or perhaps it has been greatly reproduced, or some large source of it has opened up and you see it everywhere. Antiques of this kind may lie on the shelves for some time. Then when all the furore has died down they will make a comeback—often at more realistic prices.

Cranberry glass has been coming over from England in the last ten years in such quantity that its popularity, among those who want only American antiques, took a nose dive for a few years. Now it is back again, more wanted than ever. The buying public has learned to accept imports. But what is more significant, they have learned to distinguish the good cranberry from the inferior, no matter what its origin. Bisque went into a decline for a while because people got tired of the Victorian pieces, most of them of poor quality. But it is back, carried along by the importations of fine French, English, and German pieces, and so bisque prices are going up. Interest dropped in milk glass for a time when the flood of reproductions first hit the shops. Many dealers were afraid to carry it because it was frequently difficult to distinguish the new from the old. Now it is back again. Buyers have been studying it and are learning to look for the unusual pieces that have not been reproduced. At the moment there is a lull in the buying of English luster, but there is no reason why this attractive ware should stand still. A large quantity of it was brought over a few years ago, and interest declined, but it will come back in favor when the importations are absorbed and there is less of it in the shops.

Price, quality, and artistry aside, often simple personal preference dictates a sale when a buyer enters a shop overwhelmingly filled with these late antiques. It is like visiting a foreign country without a Baedecker or guide. The buyer wanders around until he finds something he *likes*. Of course this is a good reason for buying anything, but it often results in a costly mistake, such as buying a modern pewter inkwell at a 19th-century price. If a buyer wants to get his money's worth and come out the door with something that is worth keeping over the years, a little knowledge is as good an asset as the money in his purse.

It is to promote this knowledge that this book has been written. It aims to give some status to the antiques of fifty to seventy-five years of age, to sort out the chaff from the grain, to point out where value lies, and to guide the collector who must limit his buying to these more available and less expensive antiques now on the market.

CHAPTER 3

FURNISHINGS

I N the first quarter of the 20th century there was little inno-
vation in furniture design in the United States. The average
home showed no signs of conscious arrangement. Things didn't
hang together in a planned way, as they do today. The person
who hired a decorator was exceptional. It was Elsie de Wolfe,
long a resident in Europe and an admirer of 18th-century
styles, who gave the business of home decorating a status in
this country. After she paved the way, young women flocked to
it as a career; it was ladylike. A whole new world of chintz and
cheerful appointments for less formal rooms began to open up
as women flocked into the field. But except in new houses, the
"parlor" didn't change much for some years. The family room
or "rec" room or den began to appear widely only from about
1930, to take the brunt of family living and keep the children
out of the rest of the house.

In these years imported pieces were valued but often were used haphazardly without benefit of a decorator. Most people made do with what they had inherited or made occasional splurges into the furniture vogues of the moment. Much of the Victorian hung over in the furnishings of the early 1900's home. A typical bedroom might have a set of a double bed, a bureau, a washstand, and a rocker in bird's-eye maple or in the elegant Circassian walnut. Young marrieds sometimes invested in an iron or brass bed instead of using the overpowering walnut one they had been born in. Dining-room furniture, if new, was probably of golden oak, lighter in construction but almost as ornate as the late Victorian pieces.

Floors were carpeted heavily for winter while "druggets" of sturdy cloth, or strips of straw matting, were substituted for summer use. The carpets were beaten by hand outdoors on a line before being tacked down again. I can remember that tea leaves were saved in our home, to be sprinkled on the carpet before sweeping to keep down the dust. In the better homes, parquet wooden floors, especially in the parlor, were covered with Oriental rugs. In a corner or embrasure of the parlor there was apt to be a cozy-corner consisting of a low couch piled with fancy cushions Eastern style, draped with curtains that were held back by crossed spears in Turkish fashion. Imagine such a thing in an American home! It may have been a hold-over from a Victorian period in the late 1800's when Turkish styles in furniture were inspired by the opening of the Suez Canal. But however it came about, the cozy-corner was quite a fad in the first years of the 1900's. A likely guess is that it was tolerated because it made a dim and comfortable place for courting couples.

But probably the most drastic change from the Victorian was *L'Art Nouveau*. We hear a lot about it now. This move-

ment, which began in Belgium and France, was a sort of rebellion on the part of artists and designers against the stilted
and overembellished forms that persisted until 1900. It was an
argument for simplicity, at least the kind that is met in natural forms. Designs for everything—pottery, glass, fabrics, lamps,
and furniture—took on swirls and curves with foliage that
showed sinuous stems, waves, wings, maidens with flowing hair,
and other such undulating lines. It had a bit of the feeling of
old Japanese designs. It was a romantic turn of expression and
flourished to a greater extent in France and England than in
America. There was less of it in furniture than in other household items. Much of it was in brass or iron, which could be
shaped into the interlaced and flowing stems of plants and
flowers. Sometimes the metal furniture was painted in color.
Don't worry too much about Art Nouveau beds or tables or
chairs. You won't find many, but at least it is a good thing to
recognize the style if you do; it is valuable today. There were
more Art Nouveau pieces among the accessories: lamps, vases,
ornaments, and the like. This influenced home styles for some
time, roughly from 1890 to 1914. A whole new conception in
American pottery was inspired by it (*see* Rookwood, Chapter
5), while much of the art glass (*see* Chapter 4) was Art Nouveau
in style, especially Tiffany's.

One novelty of the early 1900's was *Mission* furniture. Some
say it was the outgrowth of this same Art Nouveau movement
because it, too, stressed simplicity, though the stark, straight
lines of Mission had nothing in common with the swirling,
drooping designs of the French movement. Mission seems more
closely related to the American arts and crafts movement that
began in 1900. In fact, a book published in 1910 by the Popular Mechanics Company was advertised as giving full plans and
instructions for making your own Mission-style furniture.

There was little beauty in it. In comparison with other furniture made in the same period, it was the worst. Fortunately the style did not last long, nor did it spread too far. It was designed for the new bungalow type of house and was an attempt to imitate the Spanish mission furniture used in the early settlements of the West Coast. It was not made there, however, but in Binghamton, New York. It was bulky, straight-lined, strong, and functional. The solid oak boards were put together to stay; leather or burlap cushions took a lot of wear. There is not much of it around now, most of it probably finished out its life in the new recreation rooms or in summer cottages when it was discarded in favor of the fad for overstuffed sets for the living room that followed Mission.

An important influence on American furnishings in this period was a man named Elbert Hubbard. This colorful figure started out in the soap business in Chicago. Later, imbued with the esthetic principles of William Morris in England, he set up his own artist colony in East Aurora, New York, and called his workers Roycrofters. Here, arts and crafts were encouraged, resulting in the handcrafting of fine furniture in curly maple, mahogany, and oak. He also instituted a printing press and a book bindery. He was the author of many articles and booklets expressing his philosophy and his views of the times. He devoted his later years to writing; *A Message to Garcia* is probably the piece by which he is best known. He went down on the *Lusitania* in 1915, but he left a decided imprint on the arts and tastes of the country in the first years of the century. The growth of vocational schools and adult classes in such fields as weaving, caning, and ceramics can be traced back to his Roycrofters. Just recently the furnishings of the famous Roycroft Inn, at East Aurora, Hubbard's home and workshop, were auctioned off and presumably put a lot of this craftsman's work on the market.

William Morris, who set Hubbard on the way to his great adventure, was a pioneer of the late 1800's in an age still devoted to the Victorian. This British printer, artist, writer, and socialist was an admirer of Ruskin and his Gothic adaptations. The late Victorian Eastlake style, straight and angular, is indirectly credited to Morris, but he went much farther. An admirer of the fine craftwork of the Middle Ages, he was the exponent of the designer-craftsman approach to the making of artistic things for the home, which developed into the arts and crafts movement in this country. He established his own decorating business, which made stained glass, wallpaper, carpets, and furniture, and helped to lift the tone of Victorian furnishings in the last years of that era. Perhaps his best-known claim to fame is the Morris chair, which was named for him. While this comfortable, adjustable chair was in use before 1900, it had a long life and up until World War I was a standby in almost every American home.

A type of furniture that still survives and is now being resurrected from attics and second-hand shops is what was known at the time as *cottage* furniture. It embraced all the willow, wicker, and rattan pieces reserved for summer use in vacation houses. It was informal and cool. Much of it was imported from China and the East, as it still is today. In a way it was by far the finest of 20th-century furniture, especially in the better pieces. There were, of course, many cheap willow pieces on the market that probably did not hold up long, and there was over-elaboration in the designing. But all in all, cottage furniture had much to endear it to decorators today, to such an extent that it is being widely reproduced.

Furniture of wicker, rattan, bamboo, and what was known

as Chinese linen pieces, all woven from native reeds and shoots, were made in China where patient workmanship, expressed in styles of good taste, resulted in furniture that really was worth more than the few months of use at seashore or mountains to which most of it was delegated. The English knew its value and appreciated it after years spent abroad in their Eastern colonies. I've always wanted a lovely fan-back chair or peacock chair, as it is sometimes called. They have such dignity and grace; any woman can feel like a queen or at least a dowager in one. And they do fit into almost any room in the modern house. You can find some old ones in good condition for about $60 or a bit more. In a small garage antiques shop in New England I recently came upon two that I was forced to pass up because there was no way of getting them home in my small sedan. They, too, are being well reproduced and I may have to settle for a new one.

Another type of furniture in this cottage group was called *prairie grass*. This was American. It had the look of old Indian baskets and was woven from grasses grown in Minnesota or Wisconsin, but it was made on Long Island. Old pieces of this type usually show signs of wear. Another American-made type of summer furniture was that fashioned from swamp cedar or hickory, often with the branches left in their natural forms. You might almost call such pieces the "primitives" of the 1900's. They never wore out and are still around for those who admire them or need sturdy outdoor furniture. They were hard and unyielding and human bodies used to foam rubber and relaxing lines will probably not find them comfortable even though they are nostalgic.

When new pieces were bought for the home in the first quarter of the century, they usually came from Grand Rapids, Michigan. This city, once an Indian trading post, grew rapidly, until in 1850 it established itself as a furniture-making city, supplying not only the Midwest but the whole country. It was a natural development; logs could be floated down the rivers from the forests just north to supply its great demand for wood. This is something I was part of; my mother's family were pioneers in Michigan territory, and the small town they wrested from the Indians also became a small center for woodworking. One uncle established a fine piano factory there and most of my mother's friends were lumber entrepreneurs of some importance.

Because *Grand Rapids* furniture was made in great quantity and priced for the average buyer, the epithet "Grand Rapids style" was usually uttered with a lifting of eyebrows by those who still clung to the idea of fine pieces that showed individual workmanship. It was sold in department stores and through the mail-order houses. It was the furniture of the masses, sometimes good, often just cheap and bad.

Around 1900 there began the first widespread timid flutterings of an awareness of "antiques," real ones. A recognition of period styles began to take hold even among the uninitiated. Consequently, there was a lot of furniture made in period styles like Queen Anne, Hepplewhite, and Sheraton, but especially Chippendale. I'm sure a lot of people did not know what they were buying except that they were usually good pieces. These, what we call today *"early reproductions,"* were very good; mixed in with real antiques today, they could pass for the "real thing," except to the practiced eye of the connoisseur. They are good buys and bring good prices. A Chippendale chair in this class could bring $60 or even more. Originally they were cheap as compared with today's prices for the same kind of thing. A tilt-top table of birch, stained to look like mahogany, with authentic lines, sharply carved ball-and-claw feet, and a good one-piece dish-edge top was bought in a department store by my family in 1910 for $16! I still have it, in good condition, but worn enough to look even more like a true antique.

But the market also featured poor imitations that incorporated glued-on carving, thin wood, and inferior construction. Those pieces that did not disintegrate and are still around are not worth buying. They constitute a large part of the stock of junk shops.

In reading the catalogs of the big auction houses and galleries you can note how carefully the compilers word their descriptions for the periods in which furniture can be authenticated. They will give country and dates, but for later pieces that look genuine but made probably after 1900 they will say nothing more than "Chippendale style" or "Sheraton style," which means a fairly modern piece no matter how well it might have been made. A lot of these good reproductions are coming out of the old houses and may easily be mistaken for genuine.

There were also reproductions of French furniture, pieces reminiscent of Louis XVI, bergères, fauteuils, occasional tables, and so on, some very good and worth buying today if you fancy the French styles. But one type of pseudo-elegant parlor furniture that survived for a time was a bad imitation of the French. It had heavy frames of "mahoganized" wood and was upholstered in delicate brocades. It usually sold in sets of three, a sofa and two chairs. These are scarcely worth the notice if found today. They mean nothing, for they are not truly French reproductions nor even well-made American.

Furniture at the turn of the century was supplemented with many built-ins. Among these were wardrobes; china closets; storage spaces under windows, stairs, or in embrasures; desks and other cabinets; and folding beds. The folding bed, not a new idea by any means, went through a stage of looking like something else, often a wardrobe. Its last step was the Murphy bed, made to disappear entirely out of sight into a closet and used for small apartments and hotel rooms. None of these built-ins have much value today as new antiques unless it is for the wood from which they were made.

With the advent of electricity, home lighting obviously had to change. Table lamps with gas hose and Welsbach burners (the invention of an Austrian chemist in which an asbestos mantle with a delicate filament was heated to incandescence to give a strong, steady light) were replaced by ornate electric lamps. The glass shades large enough to shield the gas flame gave way to smaller ones to hide the electric bulb on chandeliers and wall sconces (*see* photo section). All these glass shades are desirable today for use in converting and making new lamps. As electric wiring became more advanced, more lamps could be used in one room. The center ceiling light was retained for the living room and dining room, but electrified. Chandeliers burst into Art Nouveau showers of glass flowers, four, five, or six arms, each capped with a lovely small shade, often petaled or paneled. Some of the finest art glass was used for these shades (*see* Chapter 4). Dome lights over the table for reading or dining replaced the Victorian oil lamp with its dripping prisms and chains that could be raised or lowered by a pulley arrangement from the ceiling.

Tiffany, from his experience in making stained-glass windows, created many of these center lights by piecing colored glass fragments together and leading the joints. Most of his dome lights were signed, but his work is so superior that it is easily recognized. He had many imitators, of course. Right now a Tiffany or Tiffany-type dome light is the biggest thing on the market. As late as two or three years ago you could scarcely give them away. Today glass domes run $75 to $150 even if not signed Tiffany. Many table lamps with brass or bronze bases and leaded glass shades were also made by Tiffany and his imitators (*see* photo section).

Mirrors were for the most part built into the furniture, whether sideboard, bureau, wardrobe, or whatever. A pier glass might still be found between the windows but it was not so fanciful as the earlier gold-framed Victorian mirror. The bedroom often contained a cheval glass that swung in a frame to give a full-length view of the figure. In the hall a three-part mirror with swinging sides made it easy for a lady to adjust her hat and veil.

This period is sometimes called "the lace curtain years"; almost every window seemed to be covered with glass curtains made of lace. They varied all the way from curtains of real French laces to bobbinet, a cotton machine-made lace with hexagonal weave that imitated the old bobbin or pillow lace. The cheapest were the Nottingham curtains, in which the lace pattern was woven in one piece on a machine. Swiss embroidery was good, as it is today. Clean, white lace curtains were a housewife's pride, but they were laundered at the cost of many pricked fingers. I know. Twice a year, the curtain frames were brought down from the attic, screwed together, and set up in the back yard where the heavily starched curtains were stretched over nails in the framework to dry. This insured perfect dimensions and did away with ironing. What you will do with old lace curtains if you find any worth saving I don't know. Or with the frames, except to use them for stretching the burlap for your hooked rugs. It would be a shame to discard really good lace; perhaps they can be used as tablecloths or at the windows again for that room with the Edwardian look.

There was not much to be said for the draperies of that period. They varied from brocades to velvets, to velours and plush—all dust catchers. When the lace curtains disappeared, the more practical and informal cretonne and chintz draperies came in, along with scrim and ruffled muslin for the windows.

A lot of handwork was done in those first years of the 1900's. Before they started knitting for the soldiers, most women had a favorite form of needlework. A woman carried a bag of "fancywork," ready to pull out during a gossip session. One of the most popular pieces was the centerpiece for the dining-room table, which was laid right on top of the white damask cloth. Embroidery patterns were worked in colorful silks and shaded to give realistic effects to things such as flowers, butter-flies, and fruits. We had a champion embroiderer in our family, Aunt Mary Smith. Yes, that was really her name! Her specialty was strawberries, luscious ones of scarlet silk stitches. What I would give for one of her strawberry centerpieces today! I would frame it and value it as I would an early sampler or a fine needlepoint picture.

Openwork that resembled the white Madeira embroidery found in imported linens was another favorite kind of pick-up work. Busy fingers crocheted yards of "filet" lace, a square mesh with patterns, for towels and cloths, while others turned out Irish crochet for trimming their blouses and lingerie. They also made Battenburg or Renaissance lace by joining cotton or linen braid with lace stitches to form patterns. It was used lavishly on scarves and tablecloths that are showing up in the shops right now but bringing only $5 to $10 a piece. When I think of the hours that went into their making this seems almost like an insult.

I was rich in aunts with nimble fingers. Aunt Kate, the lily-of-the-field in my mother's family, justified a sort of semi-invalidism by turning out masterpieces with her needle and making the best angel-food cakes in town. I still have a crocheted bedspread done in "popcorn" stitch that is just as good as the day she passed it on to me as a wedding gift.

From this general sketch you can get a picture of what the interiors of our houses looked like at the turn of the century. Many of the articles I have described were finally sold to the junkman but are now turning up in the antiques shops. Many pieces of this period lend themselves to conversion to a new use; few when found can be used as is. They are not intended to look old-fashioned or antique so much as interesting. Young people who cannot afford new pieces, even the reproductions that are often very good but not cheap, are picking up these new antiques here and there, cutting them down, removing the jimcracks, refinishing, antiquing and painting them to turn them into useful but interesting pieces with a flare. It's fun to do; it also saves money. You can find many such discards by haunting the thrift shops and the Salvation Army stores. That big, round table is pretty awful, you think, but those four carved legs would make wonderful lamp bases, painted white, touched up with a little gold or antiqued by rubbing on a little burnt umber and as quickly rubbing it off again. Topped with gold paper shades they will look as if they had just come out of a decorator's atelier.

But it is really the decorators who are the best customers for the junk, second-hand pieces and items in the charity outlets. Ever since it has been pontifically decreed by the best decorators that styles can be mixed—if you know how to do it— furniture of all woods, styles, and origins are finding strange bedfellows in modern homes. Right now the decorators are welcoming the Edwardian. It is something different from the overworked Victorian and the cold, uninspiring modern. Dec-

orators who cannot find old pieces are picking up the reproductions. The pages of the home and women's magazines are
full of pictures showing brass beds, wicker chairs, bentwood
furniture, and such, worked in with more modern pieces to
offer variety and distinction to interiors. While no one yearns
for the Victorian clutter, many people today, in search for in-
dividuality, have a craving for unusual pieces that will give
personal qualities to their rooms. Many of these can be found
among the cast-offs of the last generation or generations. The
"camp" shops are places to investigate.

These new antiques can be used in ingenious and outstanding ways. An old porch swing, for instance, dug from a dark
corner in a junk pile can be upholstered and swung on chains
from the ceiling in place of a sofa. It is quite in line with the
new all-out hanging chairs. Four solid wooden shutters from
the same junk source are hinged together and painted or decorated with prints to do the same job as a priceless Coramandel
screen. A large coffee canister from an old store is decorated
to make a colorful end table. That marble washstand built
into a bedroom in the late 90's now finds itself transplanted
to a powder room and newly encased. The clothes tree or cos-
tumer blooms with hanging plants or holds towels in a re-
modeled bathroom. Buggy steps become a plant stand or are
turned to use in the study or library or even the kitchen for
reaching high shelves.

A small trunk or foot locker can be covered with gay paper
and used with a glass top for a coffee table. A small brass fender
can be featured on a window sill for hiding a row of potted
plants. Tops of newel posts make fine lamp bases. One ingenious dealer paints those with globe tops to resemble the old
bonnetieres, with their slick hair and doll faces, and sells them
for hat stands. Some decorators are making acceptable end

tables from old radio cabinets, victrolas, and spool cases by putting them on new legs or cutting them down to the right height. All kinds of old cabinets are in demand, those from doctors' and dentists' offices, as well as the more familiar apothecary chests, for storing or displaying small collectibles, or, when the shelves are removed, for storing old guns. Do not despise the old treadle sewing machine. It has many uses. The iron base with treadle removed and a new top of wood or marble makes a fine table for patio or terrace. The top cover, if it was an essentially good one, can be reversed and lined with copper for use as a floor planter.

Decorators are really ingenious these days about planters; they are adapting all kinds of things to hold greenery. Bird and parrot cages, painted or gilded, are filled with trailing vines. Old battery jars also make fine planters or even small aquariums. Crocks, bushel measures, sap buckets, slop jars from bedroom sets, on the other hand, make practical and interesting waste baskets. As for lamps, almost anything can turn up as a lamp base. The tendency to be too "cute" should, however, be curbed and things of value should not be ruined in the conversion. The best way to treat a fine vase, figurine, or pitcher is to buy one of the available electrified units and simply rest the antique piece on the small stand against the pipe that holds the wiring. A small wicker basket may be turned upside down for a practical lampshade or reversed for reflected lighting. Old-timers will remember the Japanese paper lanterns that used to illuminate every strawberry festival. The best of them at the end of a hanging electric bulb are very like some of the new fixtures and much more original.

Wall treatments often replace pictures in a decorator's scheme. A number of related or unrelated objects will be gathered together on one wall and placed in some geometric arrangement. Or small items will be arranged on a board or panel into a sort of *nature morte* or still life. Beveled panels from old doors at the hands of a good artist make most effective decorative wall treatments and bread boards are being bought up by the painters of primitives. Pieces of discarded furniture can yield carvings to be used as wall pieces. At every sale there is a buyer for these bits, which cost from 50 cents to $1. Parts from old weathervanes, large gilded letters from old signs, a spread of old playing cards, cookie cutters, keys, clock hands, pin cushions, the binding of an old book—all may be used in a composition on a wall. It is an interesting way of preserving the bits and pieces left over from an earlier day.

A favorite arrangement for a kitchen is the grouping of simple wooden utensils on a board: spoons, paddles, forks, rolling pins, even glove stretchers and stocking stretchers. The whole is given a new finish of wax or stain or varnish to make a sort of primitive still life.

Room dividers can be fashioned from the most amazing things, a row of buggy whips, parts of old bead portieres, a length of iron fence, for instance. They all fit into the off-beat effect that the decorators find challenging at the moment. Little of this kind of thing will last; one tires of it quickly. But it is not intended to be permanent. However, here and there a good decorator will find a newly old piece that will prove satisfying enough to stay and be passed on.

Here are some of the furnishings from the turn of the century that you may find hiding in your attics or cellars or offered in the shops today:

China closets on legs with glass doors and side panels (not the old corner or wall-type cupboards) usually matched the dining-room set. A few years ago they were a drug on the market and could be picked up at sales or in junk shops for a few dollars. Now they are getting hard to come by. More people, dealers as well as their customers, are finding them valuable as display cabinets for small collectibles. They are even coming back into the dining room for showing up fine china. When treated by cutting down the legs, painting, lacquering, or antiquing, they can be made to fit into almost any setting. They are a good buy. If you can find one for $15 or $20 you are doing well.

Piano stools from the turn of the century, those with revolving seats, adjustable for height, make handy stools for a desk, a dressing table, or in the kitchen. They often were sold with the piano. It is said that by 1905 there was a piano in almost every home; people scrimped for one as they do today for a TV set. The stools that went with them usually had ball and claw feet, often of brass grasping a glass ball. They are more usable than the earlier ones because they were not so ornate. Piano benches can be dressed up with new upholstery or a cushion and the wood refinished or painted to serve as extra seating in modern rooms. Or they can be cut down to coffee-table height.

Revolving bookcases are handy pieces of furniture and deserve a longer life than promised in the early years of their use. The one objection is that they take up more room than bookshelves. But they can be used as end tables if they are not too high. It is significant that they are being reproduced right now.

Onyx tables were popular parlor pieces at the turn of the century. They were stands of brass with onyx tops designed to hold a plant, a piece of statuary, or a piano lamp. They are being resurrected and are widely sold in the antiques shops. I'd suggest avoiding them unless your furnishings are in the grand manner or have some French leanings. I can't see any way to make them fit in with a casual interior.

Hatracks, a hangover from the Victorian years, were still around in 20th-century homes and can be picked up in the second-hand shops unless someone has beat you to it. They were usually monstrosities of bad taste, yet ingenious things are being done to make them acceptable in the modern home. They make excellent plant stands for a patio or porch, especially the iron ones; when made of wood, the superfluous carving and useless shelves can be removed to turn them into handy pieces in a hall or beside a front door. Painting will cover a multitude of sins.

Ice-cream parlor sets, consisting of a table and four chairs, in iron or wood, are riding the wave of popularity at the moment and bring far more than they are worth. The bent and twisted iron wire pieces usually had plywood seats, occasionally with a marble top for the round table. They are found usually in two patterns, loop-back and heart-back, the latter being more preferred. In good condition they are easily repainted for breakfast sets or patio meals. However, for the same amount of money—chairs run $10 to $15 each, tables up to $50—you can buy a set of new, well-designed iron furniture in any department store. This is a prime example of a fad that was sensible enough when these pieces could be found at a bargain price, but now is an expensive whim.

Chifferobes were an integral part of a bedroom "suite" in the early 1900's. It was a version of His and Hers; she had the bureau and he had the chifferobe. This was an adaptation of the chiffonier, the traditional tall chest of drawers in which the French ladies kept their odds and ends of needlework. In France they were beautifully made of fine woods, mahogany, rosewood, or ebony. Some versions of them were made in the various periods that followed. We had chiffoniers, too, but the chifferobe, with its mirror, shelves, drawers, and a cupboard for suits, was much smarter in the 1920's. They are usable today if the wood is good. Built into a closet or small embrasure, they often make a fine dressing corner for the man of the house.

Bentwood furniture had its beginning in this country as early as 1860. Chairs of bentwood were called "Vienna chairs" because they were made by an Austrian, Gebrueder Thonet. This departure from the traditional wooden construction persisted well into the new century. Several American firms made them, too. The wood, usually ash, was steamed and bent into flowing lines and curves, and was painted black or made to look like mahogany. It echoed the feeling of Art Nouveau perhaps more than other furniture. It would be hard to find anything more pleasing or more comfortable than a "ladies' rocker" in bentwood (*see* photo section). These chairs had one piece of wood that curled over to form arms as well as the rockers that tilted back far enough to make a sort of chaise longue or contour chair. Bentwood was used for many cheap chairs in shops and offices. It has only recently come to the attention of the decorators who find it useful and compatible with many other furnishings. It is being made again today, but the old, authentic pieces have a special mellow charm.

Gas logs were a popular home accessory at the turn of the century. They had a great vogue in houses where small Victorian fireplaces still existed, particularly those that had marble mantles in the parlors. A wood fire on the hearth went out of mass fashion when central heating came in and copious domestic help disappeared, too. It was too much trouble to carry in the logs, make the fires, and remove the ashes, especially in city houses. It was some years again before the open fire on the hearth was appreciated and enjoyed enough to be worth the trouble. Around 1915 to 1920 new houses had begun to have practical fireplaces that were designed for cheery log fires. But in the meantime gas logs had been installed in fireplaces all over the country. These really were a neat little pile of asbestos-covered "logs," with vents for the gas flames, that gave the semblance of an open fire and warmth if needed. In England they still use them in houses without central heating. In American houses built just before and after 1900 where gas pipes are still present they can still be used but are not too easily built into rooms of later vintage.

Clocks of marble, ormolu, and onyx were the fashionable things to have on the mantle in these early years. Because the old shelf clocks of Terry, Seth Thomas, Chauncey Jerome, and others are getting harder and more expensive to find, many people are turning to these late ones and having them put into running order. Another type occupying the attention of the collectors of the unusual is the china clock. This was usually a boudoir piece, dainty and colorful, and was often made and signed by the foreign china factories. Many are signed Bonn (*see* German china, Chapter 5), others Dresden and Haviland. But the works were usually American-made at the Ansonia clockworks in Connecticut. These will run over $50 if in working order, and do not have to be confined to bedroom use. *Cuckoo Clocks* are having a healthy revival. They have been made for years in the Black Forest, where native craftsmen turned out beautiful specimens of fine carving and mechanism. They were fashionable from 1905 to 1915. Those made today do not have the quality of the old ones, which can run in price from $35 to $50. Many of the Seth Thomas clocks made up to 1920–1925 are of good enough quality to make them worth buying and putting into running order if necessary. They are simple in line and very appropriate with today's furnishings. Interest in old clocks at the moment stops with the electric clock, which appeared as early as 1914, and by the 1920's was going full speed ahead.

Pictures. There is such an insatiable demand now for oils that almost anything "hand-painted" does not stay long in a shop, and a lot of trash has been dug up to fill this demand. Here is where good taste and discrimination count; a good print is better than a bad painting. To some people all that matters is that a picture is actually painted by hand. Often the frame is worth more than the canvas. A great number of oils were produced around the turn of the century, many unsigned, probably the work of students or amateurs, and hung with pride on family walls. Some were undoubtedly mass-produced. I don't know how many of you readers ever saw the little man in a blue smock who used to sit in a window on Lexington Avenue in New York years ago, all day long painting one picture after another, usually landscapes as alike as peas in a pod. They were no worse and no better than the ones that now fill many shops. Yet once in a while you can come upon a gem in this welter of the commonplace. So it is well to keep looking at what the antiques dealers have to offer. If you know something of the art of the period you may be able to spot things the art dealer has missed.

Many desirable paintings were produced before and after the turn of the century. The names from these years that have become important to art dealers, but which are not likely to show up among the antiques, are Winslow Homer, William Harnett, Thomas Eakins, John Sloan, George Bellows, and many more. But there are two essentially of their times that the antiques world seems to have taken to its heart: Frederic Remington and Charles M. Russell, both portrayers of the

West. To Remington's perceptive eye we owe our modern conception of what the West was like in the 80's and 90's. It is possible that the gold rush to the Klondike in 1897–1898 spurred interest in the Old West of the California gold-rush days fifty years earlier. Remington lived on the Western plains and his pictures are as lifelike as his art could make them. He did many magazine illustrations, and it is supposed that he turned out thousands of Indians, broncos, soldiers, and cowboys, so there are still quite a few of his sketches and finished pictures around. He also was a sculptor, and it is thought that his bronzes are better than his paintings; replicas of his twenty-three bronzes are in museums and private collections. To find and be able to afford an original Remington would be a triumph indeed. But his sketches occasionally turn up in odd places where they can be picked up for purchase.

In the houses of the early 1900's, the Currier and Ives lithographs were being replaced by several different things. One was the tinted photographs of Wallace Nutting, who glorified the antique interiors, the stone walls, and the orchards of New England. Yes, this is the same Wallace Nutting who wrote the magnificent *Furniture Treasury*, a standard reference in the antiques field. His photos were probably the first to be used as pictures for the wall. They are more nostalgic than artistic. Photography has made such strides as a form of artistic expression that these first examples seem pallid to the modern eye, even when tinted. But they are being sold in the antiques shops and are quietly bought up by collectors, probably in much the same way that Harry Peters, the famous authority on Currier and Ives, first bought his prints over sixty years ago. All of these art forms were among the last gasp of "representationalism" that preceded the mass interest in contemporary art. There are many who will hold to them stubbornly in the face of the concern for op, pop, constructions, abstract expressionism, and other new forms.

An artist who left an impact on the first years of the century, in a slightly different way, was Maxfield Parrish (born in 1870). He was the son of an artist and became an illustrator and mural painter. His work appeared in children's books, on magazine covers, in catalogs, and on calendars; and his pictures were mass-produced and distributed widely. Of his dramatic murals, the mosaic in the Philadelphia building of the Curtis Publishing Company, often reproduced, is the best known; it probably did more than anything else to make his work familiar to two generations of Americans. Entitled "The Dream Garden," it is a tremendous piece, fifteen by forty-nine feet; in its idealized scene, trees, foliage, mountains, canyons, and waterfalls all show the unmistakable Parrish touch, not like anything done before or since. Parrish's colors always sang with brilliance; he used a distinctive bright blue that came from a special imported pigment containing lapis lazuli. His subjects had a dreamy, fairy-tale quality with graceful girls looking like medieval pages, playful children, glowing landscapes, even dragons and giants. Though very popular in his time, Maxfield Parrish has not yet been taken up by this generation. You don't see his pictures around in the antiques shops but you will, or I miss my guess. They are worthy of collecting as true examples of the Art Nouveau movement.

CHAPTER 4

GLASS

I N glass, perhaps more than in anything else, the period just before and after 1900 was noteworthy. In this area there is real reason for the collector to rejoice when he finds the things that undoubtedly deserve the name antique. Except in rare instances, glass from this time has quality and will continue to please generations to come. Some of the finest glass in our history was made in these years. In fact, the glass at the turn of the century climaxed the output of the 19th century, which has been called the golden age of glassmaking. No wonder this late glass is being collected so avidly. From 1890 on, art-glass creations developed in variety and new skills, cut glass began what is called its Brilliant Period, pressed glass came out in many new patterns, while many fine imports from England, France, Italy, Austria, and Bohemia, swelled the supply in this country. These decades coincided with the Art Nouveau movement described in the last chapter; glass perhaps more than any other category of antiques reflected its character.

Art Glass

At the moment there is more activity in art glass than in other varieties, in spite of its high prices. Art glass was a "fancy glass," usually colored. Glassmakers, both here and abroad, seemed to bring their highest skills to the making of it. Interest in it has mounted within the last decade; before that, it was considered by the uninitiated simply the showy old glass that grandmother used to display on her parlor mantle or in the corner whatnot. Prices do not seem to be based on rarity, for there is still plenty of it around. In fact when I meet whole shelves packed with glowing examples of the many varieties of this glass, I can't help wondering where it all comes from or where the average collector finds the money to buy it so steadily. Several pieces of Burmese would buy a good used car or keep a boy or girl in college for a year. Yet this collecting does not seem to be a rich man's hobby. I was amazed when a man of modest means, a junior executive in a big mill, told me he is collecting Amberina, which can run to $100 or more a piece, and in the plated Amberina (with a fiery opalescent lining to the ribbed amber-to-ruby outer layer) to over $1000. I assume, naturally, that his collection would run to more than two or three pieces. Yet this category and all others in art glass is being bought in quantity in spite of the prices. I suspect that a collector in this field has no other vices, that his budget for entertainment and self-improvement is low. Perhaps his wife does not mind wearing four-year-old coats, his taste buds have not been cultivated to demand gourmet food, and dancing and music lessons for the children are considered superfluous.

Something has to give in the face of such a hobby. However, one perfect piece of Mt. Washington Peachblow can be a joy forever and is not beyond the hopes of many of us.

This type of glass is usually called Victorian or Nineteenth Century, because much of it began to be made in the 1880's and was popular at the end of the Victorian era. Many varieties, however, are true turn-of-the-century antiques, though some of this glass was made as late as the 1930's. Informed collectors are familiar with the 19th-century names: Peachblow, Mother-of-Pearl, Satin, Coralene, Amberina, Burmese, Agata, Pomona, Crown Milano, Albertina, Pelaton, Vasa Murrhina, Tortoise Shell, and Craquelle, all developed in less than two decades before 1900. Many of these glass varieties were not original with American glass houses, but were versions of techniques that had been tried out in other countries and in other times. Crackled glass, for instance, was a Venetian invention revived by 19th-century glassmakers. English firms like Thomas Webb and Sons, Stevens and Williams, and others, produced pieces that unless marked can easily be confused with our own glass of the same years, for American glass was as good in this field as any other. In cameo glass (not produced to any extent in America) the outstanding names are Loetz of Austria; Gallé, Daum, de Vez, of France. In fact, the whole Western world seemed to be breaking out in elegant fantasies of glass in the years between 1880 and 1910.

To confine this discussion to the art of glass made around the turn of the century, however, we must venture into what is known as *iridescent* glass. Two names stand out foremost in this field: Frederick Carder, who died in 1963 at the age of one hundred, and Louis Tiffany.

Carder, an Englishman, learned the glassmaking business early in his father's establishment. As a young man he was employed by Stevens and Williams as a designer, and in 1903 was sent by his firm to this country to study American methods. He liked America and stayed on to become a giant in American glassmaking. He founded the Steuben Glass Works in Corning, New York, primarily to make glass blanks for the T. G. Hawkes Company for cutting. But his activities did not stop there. Under his direction, Steuben was soon making colored glass, opalescent glass, and all kinds of art glass. Carder was an originator. Among his creations are Verre de Soie, Aurene, Cluthra, and sculptured glass. The Carder cult is very strong among the collectors and emphasis is given to any of his pieces that are signed or authenticated.

Louis *Tiffany,* son of the New York jeweler, established his own glass works first in Jersey City and later at Corona, Long Island, where his famous *favrile* pieces were made. His earlier excursion into glassmaking was stained glass. Many kinds of glass were marked *Favrile,* but the glass most of us recognize was the iridescent.

The technique of iridescence was inspired by the appearance of old glass that had been buried in the earth for centuries. The action of carbonic acid or ammonia salts on a moist glass surface decomposed the glass, leaving scales or irregularities that refracted the light and gave off an iridescent effect. The glassmakers, by various experiments, finally arrived at a method, or methods, that left a finely ridged or scaly film on the glass, and caused the light to break into the colors of the spectrum.

It is said that Tiffany, by means of changing the body color of the glass, was able to approximate the lovely iridescence of a peacock's tail or a butterfly's wings. He made what is called *Mohammedan blue* or *butterfly blue,* using a body of transparent blue, green, or purple before treating it to iridescence.

His glass is usually recognizable, but many followers used his methods, and unless a piece is marked it is safer to call it Tiffany-type. The marks are L. C. Tiffany, L. C. T., or Favrile. The Tiffany works produced almost everything possible to make in glass: tableware such as plates, goblets, compotes, salts, pitchers, bowls, sherbets, even cups and saucers; vases; lamps; desk sets; decanters; wines; finger bowls; nut sets; toothpick holders; tiles; fire screens; gas and electric shades; and candlesticks. One of the showpieces of the glass world is the Tiffany glass curtain made for the National Theater in Mexico City. Tiffany pieces run among the highest; a signed compote can run to $300, and even the smallest footed salt will bring $25.

Of interest to collectors, although not found to the same extent as Tiffany, is another glass with iridescent quality made by Arthur J. Nash, an Englishman, who was engaged by Tiffany in the early 1900's to run his furnaces on Long Island. His consummate skill helped to put Tiffany at the top of the list. After Tiffany's retirement in 1933, Nash and his son continued to run the plant and make iridescent glass similar to what had been made there as well as pieces characteristically their own. Nash glass is signed with the name, and not to be confused with the early Tiffany or *favrile*.

One of the finest examples of iridescent ware to be found is Aurene. It was a registered trade name of the Steuben works under Frederick Carder. It is aptly named, for it has a brilliant iridescent gold surface. Occasionally it is silvery in color. Whole pieces were made of it, and many other pieces of art glass in this period (1904) showed an aurene lining. Much of this glass is marked on the underside with a silvery fleur-de-lis, or the word Aurene, adopted by the Steuben Works for identification. It is expensive but not so high generally as Tiffany. However, because of the recent writings and publicity about

Carder, the pieces he inspired are rising drastically in price. Pieces made in Aurene were mostly decorative: vases, baskets, bowls, perfume bottles, compotes, finger bowls, and light shades, among others. Vases run $50 or $60 in price.

Verre de Soie was another Carder triumph. It was a kind of pearl satin glass manufactured first in England by Carder when he worked for Stevens and Williams, and made by him again when he came to America. It was a blown-mold, milky glass dipped in a metallic fluid to coat the outer surface and provide a sort of glass skin, which trapped air in the indentations of the blown piece. Carder called it *Verre de Soie with Air Traps*. It is a thoroughly delightful, delicate, ethereal glass with an iridescent, silky appearance produced by a metallic chloride spray. It, too, is expensive and much in demand. Around $35 will buy a sugar bowl, $45 a tall vase.

About this same time, the Quezal Art Glass Company also made a blown iridescent glass that was called simply *Quezal*. The founder of the firm, Martin Bach, was originally employed by the Tiffany plant at Corona, and used many of their techniques when he established his own factory in Brooklyn. The name Quezal (the name of a Central American bird) was registered as a trademark and appears on most pieces. It was an overlay glass of a pure, transparent color over a casing (lining) often of an Aurene type. Its distinguishing pattern is the "hooked feather," a decoration perfected by a man named Emil Larsen. Because of the great dexterity needed to achieve this feather effect, Larsen was sometimes hired by other glass houses on a free-lance basis; thus it appears on other than Quezal pieces. Often it is called Larsen glass. It was a very distinctive type of decoration, showing a peacock's eye at the tip of the feather—very handsome. It was made mostly in decorative pieces such as lamps and lamp shades, but it can often be found in bowls and small domestic items. In price Quezal compares with Aurene and Verre de Soie. A vase may cost from $35 to $50.

An offshoot of Quezal was a plant at Elmhurst, Long Island, run by Conrad Vahlsing, who engraved the word *Luster Art* on his pieces. This plant operated from 1920 to 1929.

A similar type of glass, called *Durand,* was made by Victor Durand in his factory at Vineland, New Jersey. It was a later manifestation of the kind of glass made by the Tiffany, Steuben, and Quezal companies. Pieces were marked with a large V enclosing the name Durand, or with the monogram. The plant did not close until 1930, in the depression, so that many men who worked for Durand are still living, and they can and are willing to tell you the whole Durand story. Many of them possess pieces of this handsome glass, which they display with pride. It resembled Tiffany in its golden sheen; some pieces were made in red or sapphire blue. It often used the looped design similar to the Larsen hooked feather; Larsen also worked for Durand. Prices seem to be higher than Quezal, though it is hard to say why, unless it is because there was not as much of it made. Prices run $60 to $100 a piece.

Kew Blas was a trade name said to derive from the word keweenawite, an arsenide of copper, cobalt, and nickel, the fumes of which were used to reproduce the iridescence on the glass. Blas was a coined word having to do with "an emanation from the stars," rather an elaborate way of arriving at a trademark. It was made by the Union Glass Works of Somerville, Massachusetts, in the 1890's, about the same time that Tiffany was developing his art glass. It was an opal or milk glass stained with color, then coated with clear glass, and often given an iridescence of gold or silver. There does not seem to be too much identifiable Kew Blas around. Pieces are usually marked

Kew Blas on the base, and prices run a little higher than Quezal.

Cluthra was a late glass developed by Frederick Carder, and made at the Steuben Glass works about 1925. Original examples of this glass were made thirty years earlier in Scotland, where it was called Clutha, an old Scotch word meaning cloudy. The glass was cloudy and bubbly, often showing flecks of color or mica flakes. You don't hear much of it yet, but in their pursuit of art glass in all its forms, the enthusiasts are sure to bring it to general attention, particularly since it is a Carder glass.

Carnival is often called Taffeta Glass, Cinderella Glass, or Poor Man's Tiffany. The name Carnival was given to it because it was a premium glass given away at fairs and carnivals; this is the term more generally used. Even at the time of their manufacture, all the varieties of iridescent art glass were luxury items, not cheap for the period. Too much individual skill and workmanship went into their making; they were not production-line items. It remained for a man named Harry Northwood, brother of John Northwood, a well-known glassmaker in England, to experiment with a cheaper way of making a glass with iridescence as competition with Tiffany, Quezal, and the others. The result was a pressed glass with iridescence turned out by his American factory as early as 1887. It was so cheap that it was given away with baking powder, coffee, and other grocery items. In 1910, a punch bowl with twelve cups could have been bought for $1.50! Try and get one today for less than $60. For many years Carnival lay unnoticed, considered just a cheap, showy glass that few people wanted. Today it is considered important enough for books to be written about it. (*See* Bibliography.) While some buyers scorn it, others value it highly and see beauty in it. Certainly, in some colors and forms, and in some patterns, it has a claim to due consideration. But gathered indiscriminately, it results in a collection without a great deal of distinction.

It has been established that there are more than five hundred patterns in this ware, and many people are collecting it as they have been collecting other pressed-pattern glass for years. Some are interested only in the color. Because the first pieces that came on the market were predominantly of a bright orange color, called marigold, the image created in the minds of the uninformed was that all Carnival was orange, and not an appealing one at that. Then it began to dawn upon the buyers that Carnival could be found in other colors, a rich bluish purple, amethyst, cobalt, dark green, red, light blue, and other pastels, and even white, all with iridescence. Now the hunt is on for the more unusual pieces, and surprises await the collector. One of the varieties that appeals to me is a rainbow combination of colors that resembles Tiffany except for the quality of the glass.

There are many distinctive patterns in Carnival, such as Peacock Fountain, Holly, Vintage, Dragon and Lotus, Singing Bird, Fashion, Broken Arches, but many of the familiar versions of the later pressed patterns show up in this glass.

Harry Northwood's glass was made continuously up to 1923 in his Wheeling, West Virginia, factory, which he bought in 1902 from the old firm of Hobbs Glass Company. His mark was an N on the base, and such marked pieces are usually preferred, supposedly giving the piece prestige. But many other companies quickly followed in his lead in the early 1900's, notably the Imperial Glass Company of Bellaire, Ohio, which operated from 1910 to 1920; the Fenton Glass Company of Williamstown, West Virginia; and the Millersburg Glass Company of Millersburg, Ohio. They released a flood of cheap glass-

ware that was still to be found in the five-and-dime stores up
to the 1920's.

Everything was made in Carnival glass, including sets of
bowl and cups for punch, water sets of pitcher and tumblers,
berry sets of bowl and sauce dishes, sugar-and-cream sets, vases,
hat-pin holders, dresser sets, trays, jewelry boxes, glove boxes,
powder jars, toothpick holders, candlesticks, and light shades
(*see* photo section). There is still plenty of it around but at the
rate it is being bought up, it may soon be put on the list of
rarities, as some of it already is.

This interest in fancy glass that bloomed at the turn of the
century has made important other varieties that the antiques
shows and shops are featuring today. One is *opalware*, manufactured by several different companies, of which *wavecrest* is
perhaps the one most people know best. This is blown, opaque
white glass with a stained finish, and was made by the firm of
C. F. Monroe, of Meriden, Connecticut, about 1898. This firm
got their blanks either from France, where this type of glass
originated, or from Pairpont (or Pairpoint—take your choice
of spelling!) Manufacturing Company of Bedford, Connecticut, the successor to the Mount Washington Glass Works. Apparently what Monroe did was to decorate their pieces with
flowers in the dainty Sèvres manner and sign them Wavecrest,
or with the initials of the company. In 1904, they registered
the name of Kelva for this ware, and also used the name Na-
kara, which Mr. Albert Revi, an authority on art glass, says was
never registered in Washington.

Pieces, especially the boxes, were rather bulky in shape, almost as if made from puffed satin. They were combined with
brass for rims, feet, and hinged covers; often they were satin-
lined. Wavecrest is found most often in bureau pieces such as
powder boxes, jewel boxes, hair receivers (for depositing comb-

ings), and collar-and-cuff boxes. It is also found in decorative pieces such as jardinieres, vases, humidors, desk sets, and certain household items. There is quite a demand for wavecrest now, and you will have to pay up to $50 for a box of any kind.

Opalware was not new with Monroe. The Mount Washington Glass Works patented their Crown Milano in 1893. It was also an opaque white glass, but their decorations were more elaborate, and applied by hand in enamels and gold. Their mark for this ware was a C and M, usually with a crown placed above them. Albertine was another name used by this company for a similar ware.

The Smith Brothers, an old firm of glassmakers, also of New Bedford, Massachusetts, made opalware of fine quality. Their trademark is a rampant lion. Like wavecrest, they got their blanks from the Mount Washington Works and later from Pairpont. The Smith decorations were finely executed in delicate colors; many were landscapes and pictorial subjects. Sometimes they were mounted with silverplate. They made the usual things: cracker jars, boxes, cuspidors, condiment sets, vases, and lamp shades.

Other firms put out limited supplies of this decorated opalware, and many were unmarked. The buyer is advised to look for the mark; otherwise it is a guess what you are getting. Of course, paper labels were often used, but on old pieces they have long since disappeared. Without marking, it would not be too hard to mistake the American opalware for English Bristol of the Victorian period.

Findlay Onyx Glass. The name of George W. Leighton, of Findlay, Ohio, is the one most associated with another type of art glass of the late 1800's and early 1900's. It is called onyx, a name patented by Leighton in 1889. It is just as often called Findlay glass, and is easily recognized without any marking.

By the Leighton process, a mold with raised decorations was produced in an ivory or clam-broth opaque white with an opalescence achieved by several heatings and dippings at the fluid stage. This resulted in a multilayered glass. Lusters of various kinds—silver, red, amber, orange, and purple—were achieved by various processes and showed up in patterns against the opal lining of the glass. To the nonprofessional it would seem to have been a great triumph in the art of glass-making. It had been tried and rejected by other makers of the period. It was a comparatively expensive glass in its time but it was short-lived, therefore prices today are high, running over $100 for many pieces.

Silver Deposit Glass was popular about the turn of the century, up to World War I. It was not expensive. Undoubtedly, a lot of it is lying around unnoticed in cupboards today. Until quite recently it did not receive much attention from the antique-buying public, but it has a lot to recommend it. Earlier methods of depositing silver on glass by electrolysis were complicated but the result was very handsome, especially when the glass became only a background for an elaborate all-over raised silver pattern. Later pieces, made after 1900, were more simply made, and what you usually find is of the later period, not as ornate as the early one. Moreover, it is cheap, as compared to other 20th-century glass. Many small pieces can be found for under $10.

Fostoria Iris. A late variety of iridescent glass was put out by the Fostoria Glass Specialty Company of Fostoria, Ohio, in 1912. The names Iris and Rainbow had been used for earlier sporadic attempts at making iridescent glass in this country, but it is this trademarked Iris glass of the early 1900's that concerns us. It was very close in workmanship to Tiffany and Steuben, but patterns were simpler. Much gold was used for it, some lamp shades being entirely lined with gold, like the Aurene pieces. As it was marked with paper labels, little of it can be identified. Much of the output of Iris was in shades, globes, and lamps; but it was also used for vases, bowls, finger bowls, plates, and other pieces both practical and decorative. Because it is so easily confused with Tiffany or Aurene, prices for it are apt to run high.

Foval. The firm of H. C. Fry, of Rochester, New York, established in 1900, made cut glass in its earlier years. But when that fad began to die down it turned to other types, among them a rather lovely, two-colored glass that they called Foval. It was unpatterned, made in shades of smoky blue, pink, green, and cream color. Most pieces were designed for the use of two or more contrasting colors. Thus a compote could have a pink bowl with a green base and a knob of clear glass in the stem. A few pieces were marked Fry. It was expensive to produce and perhaps not very profitable, since the firm failed in 1929. In antiques shops and ads today you will find the name of Foval mentioned at prices running up to $50. Except for some interesting combinations of color, it was far removed from the "fancy glass" at the beginning of the century.

A word here about the care of fine glass might not be amiss. It should be treated very gently, washed in lukewarm water with a minimum of suds and brushed with a very soft-bristled brush such as a baby's hairbrush. A great many pieces of colored glass have been flashed (that is, colors have been added to the clear surface, usually painted on or added in a thin layer, not incorporated with the glass mixture before firing). Such pieces cannot stand rubbing or strong detergents. Much gilt cannot take strong soap and water treatment either. The best way to treat all kinds of fancy glass is to douse it in tepid, light suds, brush softly if you must to get dirt out of crevices, rinse well, and let it drain dry. In washing clear glass a little ammonia in the water will bring out brilliance or you can use one of the special washing powders such as bars use to keep their glasses shining without drying them.

Cut Glass

The idea of cutting a design in crystal by means of a wheel and abrasive powder was not new when the vogue for cut glass began in this country just before the turn of the century. The process of decorating glass in this manner was first developed by the Romans, was rediscovered by the Germans at the end of the 1500's, was passed on to the English and Irish, and came into America late in the 1700's. Beautiful as is this early cut glass made by Stiegel, Bakewell of Pittsburgh, and others in the 1800's, it is not the concern of this book. What most buyers know today is the glass of what the authorities call the Brilliant Period, from 1880 to 1915.

Cut glass has always been a symbol of elegance, even when first made in the early years of the 19th century. Then, however, the cutting was restrained and often combined with engraving, as it was in the Middle Period (1830–1880). During that period, when tariffs were high in this country, we came to rely upon our domestic wares, but the widespread vogue for cut glass did not begin until about 1880.

Cut glass must, of course, be a heavy lead glass, sturdy enough to take the wheel. Lead glass, often called flint (or called crystal when polished with a glassmaker's soap, black oxide of manganese), had a composition of lead and silica. It was of the finest quality and used almost entirely for table ware until the Civil War when, because of the shortage of lead, a return to the old "soda glass," such as was first used early in America for bottles and window glass, was necessary. Late pressed glass was for the most part a form of soda glass, but cut glass has always been made with lead, and in the mid-1800's there was not much of that available. By 1880, however, a better quality of lead glass was perfected and cutting deep enough to give a brilliancy to the patterns was developed. Many glass houses made blanks for other factories to cut.

Cut glass required special skills, very different from the methods employed by the men who created and executed the various types of art glass. It required a fine artistic skill and a sure hand to execute the patterns. Cutters were highly paid, and the finished product was never cheap. The china closets at the turn of the century were laden with it.

Cut glass was a favorite wedding, anniversary, or special occasion gift. A housewife was not apt to go out and treat herself to expensive cut glass; she waited for it to come to her. It was the show glass of the time, reserved for company meals. I can still remember in my own home a handsome cut-glass bowl that always came to the table on Sunday nights when we had supper guests. It was filled with glowing canned quinces floating in a lovely pinkish-orange syrup, delightful to look at as well as to eat with a slice of One-Two-Three-Four cake, a kind of pound cake that it was my task to make on Saturday mornings. When the old house was finally dismantled and sold, the cut glass of generations, a barrelful of it, was given away to the cleaning woman. Where is it now? This tragedy was probably repeated countless times all over the country.

Where is all the cut glass of the 1890's and 1900's that has not been broken over the years? It is coming out of hiding and filling the counters of the antiques shops. Current generations are waking up to its value, even though most of it is too formal to mix with our more casual table settings. It went better with fine damask, gleaming silver, and elegant china. There is still a lot of it around because it was produced in great quantity at a time when this country was prosperous.

Cut glass varies in quality. The good glass was deeply cut and therefore brilliant. Shallower cutting did not give the same effect. In some instances patterns were first pressed in the blanks to give the cutters a start for their work. Today those pieces cut from partly pressed blanks are not considered top-rate. Some of the brilliance was lost because the incisions of the pressed pattern were not as sharply cut as in the best glass. The inferior cuttings are not so deep nor do they have the same sparkle. They can be spotted by examining the inside of the glass. In the later glass, the long polishing process was shortened by using a hydrochloric acid bath. Because of such short cuts that became common practice, cut glass made after 1915 became inferior. In the search for good cut glass, knowledge and discrimination help in tracing the makers and the various patterns, which can be identified through several books or articles in the antiques magazines.

There was one glass you should learn to know, not cut at all, but entirely pressed, in cut-glass patterns, often combined with a little engraving, that was made by several glass houses around the turn of the century. Some of it is so effective that it will fool the inexperienced. Run your fingers over the pattern and feel the edges. They will not be sharp or deep on the pressed glass. Pay no attention to the names such as Nu-Cut on a piece when you go to buy cut glass; this is only the name of the pattern.

Many manufacturers tried their skills at making cut glass to meet the demand of the growing market. Only the researchers have heard of many of them. But there are quite a few glass houses with names that have become synonymous with the finest in cut glass. There were T. G. Hawkes Glass Company, Libbey Glass Company, Gillinder and Sons, Dorflinger and Sons, H. C. Fry Company, Pairpont Corporation, and the Phoenix Glass Company. The Corning Glass Company did no cutting, but it made the blanks for other firms. One, J. Heare and Company of Corning, New York, did a tremendous business in cutting.

How can you and I tell the source of a cut-glass piece? In some cases they are marked by etching in acid on the base, and, of course, such marked pieces bring the higher prices. Hawkes glass was marked with the name, an H, or a trademark of two hawks in a shamrock, in recognition of Hawkes' Irish ancestry. It was Hawkes who established the Steuben Glass Company for the making of his own glass blanks. Late Hawkes pieces, from 1903 on, are acid-marked Steuben. The factory was sold to the Corning Glass Company in 1918, and is now a subsidiary of that company. One other Hawkes mark deserves mention, Gravic, used about 1900 for a steel-cutting method that resulted in a grayish floral design. It was expensive and not too much of this Gravic glass was made or is to be found today.

Fry is another name found acid-etched on cut glass. The firm of H. C. Fry made exceptionally brilliant glass at Rochester, New York, until 1929. The invention of the pressed blanks, in which Fry had an interest, was the end for him and for the whole cut-glass industry. Libbey also signed its pieces on the base with acid-etching. But most of the companies used paper labels, and of course with years of washing they are usually gone.

Some professionals can tell the maker from the quality of the glass and often by the pattern. Each firm had its own registered patterns, and some are well known enough to be recognizable. The Russian pattern, patented by Hawkes and others, is perhaps best known. It is easily the loveliest and showiest of the familiar patterns, with an overall lacy effect of small, many-faceted cut details around a central motif showing a many-pointed star or rosette. A set of fifty pieces was cut by Hawkes for the White House during Cleveland's administration. It was used throughout the Roosevelt, Taft, Wilson, and Coolidge occupancies, and has been added to and replaced from time to time. Other familiar patterns include Chair Bottom, Strawberry, and Hobstar. Stars, fans, pineapples, pinwheels, diamonds, and so on were combined in various ways, as were strictly geometric patterns. Dealers who handle cut glass have become very knowledgeable about makers and patterns, but if you want to establish a pattern or match one you already have, it is wise to consult a good book such as mentioned in the bibliography at the end of this book.

Almost every kind of article was made in cut glass: table pieces, such as plates, salts and peppers, goblets, bowls, butter dishes, sugars, creamers, water tumblers, pitchers, punch bowls, relish dishes, mustard pots, cheese dishes, cruets, compotes, nappies, decanters, bread trays, celery dishes, and finger bowls. Other items include lamps, vases, ferneries, perfume bottles, atomizers, and baskets. The small collectibles in this glass are napkin rings and knife rests that held the carving set when the roast was carved at table. (*See* photo section following page 116.)

As to prices, one thing is curious—even today, when the market is burgeoning with mounting prices in almost everything else, many cut-glass pieces do not cost as much as when they were first made. To duplicate the old pieces today, if it could be done, would double the original price, but you can still get a signed Hawkes bowl or decanter for under $50. A pair

of fine tall vases may bring $100 or more, or a punch bowl
$150. But in comparison with the original cost, they still are
not out of line. You will find, however, in some parts of the
country, particularly the South, that prices are much higher.

Late Pressed Glass

While pressed glass as a type is an early glass, beginning
about 1830, the Deming Jarves mechanical invention that
turned out the exquisite lacy glass at Sandwich helped it to
flourish throughout the whole 19th century, with the number
of patterns running well over two thousand. The glass used for
the earlier patterns was flint glass, with lead used in the composition, which gave the glass weight and brilliance. Later in
the 1800's a soda-lime glass much like the first glass made in
this country for window glass and bottles was used. It was
cheaper, and there was a shortage of lead in the Civil War years
when that metal was used for ammunition. Some patterns can
be found in both flint and soda-lime glass, but the later patterns that were produced into the 20th century were made of
the soda-lime glass.

Collectors who have come into the field lately are being
forced to look for the later patterns, since the early ones are
getting harder to find and consequently much higher in price.
A Horn of Plenty flint-glass tumbler, one of the most attractive early patterns made about 1850, will cost around $18.50,
as against a Shell and Jewel tumbler of the 1890's, which will
cost only about $3.75.

Antiques shops abound with glass that some call facetiously
"early Woolworth." It, too, is pressed, but it is usually inferior
in pressing, less sharp, and with fussy patterns. It is uniden-
tified, and naturally made to sell at a low price. After all, what

could you have expected even in those early days of the 1900's for ten cents? Here and there one can find little novelties that are quite charming, in spite of their origins, and they are worth picking up. If one does not spend too much for this late, late glass, it often makes good fillers for use with other late pieces.

There was some good pressed-pattern glass at the turn of the century. Patterns, however, were inclined to be fussy, and there was much use of red and gold flashing. Many of these patterns were named by the makers; some had only catalog numbers. If we take 1890 as the beginning of the later period, we find any number of patterns familiar to collectors, and many more that they know nothing about, which would provide them with some very nice pieces if they knew what to ask for. For instance, King's Crown was made in Marion, Indiana, in the 1890's. It is a clear glass with a deep band showing large thumbprints and often flashed with red (then it is called Ruby Thumbprint). It is very popular today. The two versions of the Dewey pitcher were made in 1898. One is called the Gridley pitcher because it bears the inscription, *Don't shoot until ready,* and shows a scroll with the names of the ships in Dewey's fleet. The other shows cannonballs, guns, the ship *Olympia,* and Dewey's face. Both are desirable items. Croesus, another very popular pattern, was produced in West Virginia in 1897 in colors as well as in clear glass. Peacock Feather (*not* the old flint Sandwich pattern) was made in Pittsburgh in the late 90's. Daisy and Button (probably with Hobnail, the most commonly reproduced of all pressed patterns) with many variants appeared well into the 1900's. Tulip Petals, a particularly lovely pattern that looked more like the early flint glass such as Argus or Ashburton with their classic plain panels, was made in 1903.

Hundred Eye was an 1890 glass. Wedding Bells, made by Fostoria in the early 1900's, was a pleasing design of scrolled lines running diagonally. It is hard to describe many of these late patterns in words. Often the names do not fit the pattern at all and even the dealers must look them up and consult the photos of them in the various books. Many are reissues of old patterns. When you hear the term *late* combined with a known name, such as Jacob's Ladder, it usually means the version reissued by a new company, who perhaps bought the old mold; this was frequently done. Moon and Star (originally made in 1874) is a popular item today, and what you will find is likely to be a variant made in the 90's by several companies. The Beaded Grape pattern, relatively plentiful today, is more likely to be the output of the United States Glass Company (it was called California in their catalog) rather than the early one made by the Boston and Sandwich Company. Current reproductions, however, cannot be called reissues. Those made in the 90's and later by the United States Glass Company and others were often made from the old molds acquired along with the patents of the parent companies.

There were a number of large companies producing pattern glass by 1900, some continuing into the 1900's. Several were combines of other companies, such as the United States Glass Company, established in 1891 with eighteen member companies. Even after the panic of 1893 and the strikes and labor troubles of the early 1890's had reduced their membership to six firms, they continued to influence the glass business for years. In its heyday, this company put out well over one hundred and fifty patterns, some new ones of their own as well as the reissues of other companies. The National Glass Company of Pittsburgh, Pennsylvania, established in 1899, was an amalgamation of nineteen companies.

The Westmoreland Glass Company, begun in 1890, was another large concern that marketed pressed-pattern glass at the turn of the century. Its milk-glass pieces were a specialty. Today this company is largely responsible for the milk glass reproductions found in the gift shops. The firm of Jefferson, in Steubenville, Ohio, made much fancy glass, but later went into the production of fine pieces of pattern glass both pressed and hand-tooled. Another large firm of the period was A. H. Heisey, with a listing of about thirty patterns, using for a trademark the letter H within a diamond. Fostoria in the 1890's put out about fifty patterns, most of which were named. This company made many of the patterns that resembled cut glass, as did many other companies just before and after 1900. They used contrived names, such as Nu-Cut (Imperial Glass Company), Pres-Cut (McKee Brothers, of Pittsburgh), Near-Cut (The Cambridge Glass Company), as well as other names like Rex, Unique, Tempee, which do not mean much to the present-day collector unless he has done his homework.

This business of names is very confusing. Sometimes when a company used only a number for a patented pattern, a name developed as it struck the market and the popular fancy. This explains why a pattern might have two names, such as occurs in many of the "states" patterns like Dakota, Delaware, Utah, Virginia, Texas, New Jersey, New Hampshire, etc. There are thirty-four patterns named after states and many of them had other names such a Beaded Dewdrop (Wisconsin); or Baby Thumbprint or Thumbprint Band (Dakota).

Probably the naming of patterns has had a lot to do with their popularity. It is easier to remember Bow Tie, which looks like the name, than Thompson's Number 18, or Paneled Forget-Me-Not than Number 24 of the U.S. Glass Company. To find your way around in this maze of names and numbers you need to consult a good book on pattern glass with photographs or drawings. I have mentioned several good ones in the bibliography at the end of this book.

One pattern deserves special mention here: Silver Age, better known as *coin glass,* made about 1892 by the Central Glass Company and the Hobbs Glass Company, both of Wheeling, West Virginia, members of the United States Glass Company combine. It was designed as a memento of the centennial of the establishment of the United States mint, and was aimed at the advocates of the free-silver campaign. Real United States coins were used as molds for the impressed motifs, but after only five months of production, the federal government stepped in and put a stop to this on the basis that it was counterfeiting—which has always seemed far-fetched to me. Today, coin glass is one of the highest-priced examples of pressed glass on the market. Goblets that once sold for $4 a dozen could now set the buyer back $100 apiece or more, a good example of what small supply does to prices. This glass is not to be confused with a very recent coin glass put out by Fostoria; the coin motifs show some changes to avoid the counterfeiting charge and have no dates. The coins used for the real thing were dollars, half dollars, quarters, and dimes. Don't worry if you see an impression of a different kind of dime; it was the Seated Liberty dime, not used after 1891.

A similar glass called *Columbian coin* or *Spanish coin,* put out by the Central Glass Company about the same time, used a pattern of South American coins. While still nowhere near the United States coin glass in price, it has become expensive, probably because there are some who do not recognize the difference. A goblet of this Spanish coin pattern will now bring $25.

A category of pressed glass called *Greentown glass* requires some explanation. This was glass put out by the Indiana Tumbler and Goblet Company, in Greentown, Indiana. This company made a number of pressed-glass patterns in clear and colored glass from 1894 to 1903, including the popular Cactus pattern, showing beaded leaves of the cactus plant. They are perhaps best noted for their caramel glass, also called chocolate, from its rich, creamy tan color. This glass, originated by Jacob Rosenthal, is opaque, related to opaque white milk glass. It was used in novelty dishes and other pieces in Cactus, Shell and Leaf, and about ten of their most desirable pressed-glass patterns. The footed dish shaped like a dolphin with two fins for the feet and a small fish for a finial on the cover is a favorite with collectors of caramel glass.

Another famous Greentown glass is Holly Amber, also attributed to Jacob Rosenthal, of that company. It is a deep amber glass with a raised holly leaf border or panels, which became opalescent on a second heating. It is unusual because both the clear amber and the opalescent milky glass are combined in one piece. It was made for about one year only, and was a casualty of the fire that destroyed the plant in 1903. For this reason the prices on Holly Amber have risen to astronomical heights, many think without reason. Only the future will tell whether they will hold up or not. A covered compote could cost $675, a small sauce dish $100. It is quality material, and it can be found but not in great quantity. There are rumors that it is being reproduced, but I have not seen any of the new. I should think it would not be hard to recognize the reproductions if you have once seen and handled the original.

You see and hear a lot about custard glass, a light, creamy yellow glass, a creation of Harry Northwood, the same one who brought out Carnival glass. Northwood made this custard glass from 1886 until 1913; some of it is marked with an N in the same way as his carnival pieces. It is a pressed pattern glass with painted decoration. You will sometimes find it plain with no pattern—to my mind handsomer than the decorated pieces —but most of it was pressed in patterns such as Argonaut Shell, Winged Scroll, Golden Daisy and Rose, and Chrysanthemum Sprig with part of the pressed design accented with painted colors, often a dark green, and a lot of gilt.

Some *milk glass* was made after 1900, but by far the most and best was made in the 1870's and 1880's. It was an opaque glass, as was *mosaic* or *marble glass,* sometimes called *slag.* All the various kinds of opaque glass were made around the turn of the century, but they do not strictly belong to the period of the early 1900's that we are discussing.

Etched Glass

About the same time that cut glass was in favor, a cheaper but not unattractive means of decoration was etching. This is not to be confused with engraved glass, which is really a shallow cutting with a copper wheel. Etching is done with acid, which eats out the pattern. It is not as deep as engraving and is usually frosted. It was often combined with pressed-glass patterns to look like cut glass. Many pieces made around 1900 were etched with delicate sprays, ferns, grapes, and banding in the Roman Key pattern. Such pieces were often the wedding glass of our grandmothers.

Imports

Much of the fine glass used around 1900 was imported. Glassmakers in England and on the continent found a good market in the United States. Much art glass, made about the same time as in our factories, came over from England, and is highly prized by collectors, especially when signed. Choice names to look for are Webb, Stevens and Williams, and Northwood (John Northwood, brother of Harry Northwood of this country). *Cranberry,* a colored glass, was another import from England that began coming over around the turn of the century and is still coming. It is very popular today. The so-called *Mary Gregory glass,* made in America at the Sandwich factory in the late 1800's, had its counterpart in English, French, German, and Bohemian wares. It was produced until 1912, and late pieces are still showing up among the imports from foreign countries.

One thing America did not make, at least in any appreciable quantity, was cameo glass. Imported pieces from 1890 on were from top European glassmakers, including the English. In France cameo glass reached its heights in the Art Nouveau period under such men as Gallé, operating in Nancy, whose pieces, showing flowers and landscapes in this beautiful layered glass cut in cameo style, were marked with his name. When he died, his successor, Victor Preuve, continued his work and marked his pieces Gallé with a star preceding the name. The Daum brothers, also of Nancy, produced this glass in the 1890's, and the firm of that name is active today. De Vez, another name you see in the advertisements of the good shops, worked near Paris in the 20th century. His cameo glass showed beautiful colors and floral designs. Le Gras worked in Saint-Denis up to 1914 and is noted for his scenic designs cut in cameo fashion. Many more names are associated with French cameo in these years, some better known than others, but all worth the attention of the collector today—if he can afford to indulge his good taste. Like all the other art glass, it comes high. Small perfume bottles of Daum-Nancy origin, or Gallé, will run to $50 or $75. A signed cameo vase will run much higher.

In Val St. Lambert, in Belgium, cameo glass under that name was beautifully executed, with cutting and engraving to get the same effect. Loetz of Austria, who made much iridescent ware at about the time of Tiffany, also made cameo glass inspired by the French designers. Pieces signed with these names are scattered throughout the better antiques shops and may even be reposing in homes where good things were bought at the turn of the century.

Another glassmaking center was in Baccarat, in France, where glass of that name has been made from 1818 to the present time. The Baccarat factory is particularly noted for its fine paperweights, made between 1845 and 1850, but the plant also made much fine tableware that has continued to this day. Some of the patterns resembled our lacy pressed-glass pieces. Glass items bearing the Baccarat name that came into the country at the turn of the century, when the finest in tableware was being sought for elegant entertaining, stand out among later glass antiques. Among signed Baccarat articles are many small pieces such as swirled amberina perfume bottles, decanters, inkwells, relish dishes and so on, many in colored glass.

Lalique has been a favorite for years. It was the work of René Lalique, who worked in Paris from 1905 to about 1930. It, too, was an elegant glass, a combination of pressing, blowing, frosting, and cutting. While Lalique made many kinds of glass, the most recognizable are the frosted pieces with figures in relief. Much of it found its way to America, and it is currently receiving much attention among dealers and collectors. You'll find it in perfume bottles, plaques, place-card holders, and vases, as well as tableware. It is noted for the purity of the glass and distinctive designs of foliage, flowers, birds, animals, and draped figures. It, too, reflects the influence of the Art Nouveau movement.

Vallerystahl, a French glass center in Lorraine, for a long time under the dominance of the Germans, was the source of much milk glass, often impossible to differentiate from our own made here in the late 1800's. It was generally signed and specialists can recognize it by its slightly grayish color. Modern pieces are coming over from Vallerystahl just as our own reproductions are appearing on the market.

Bottles

Bottle collecting has stepped up in volume in the last few years. In fact several new bottle books have appeared almost simultaneously (see Bibliography), and articles on bottles of all kinds are a steady item in the table of contents of many antiques magazines. While the greater interest used to be in blown bottles of the 18th century and in flasks (1820–1875), today's collector has gone a few steps farther and is picking up many kinds of bottles made from 1890 into the 1900's. As is the case with so many of the antiques considered in this book, this is a result of easier availability and lower prices. Generally speaking, the later bottles are cheaper than the early ones, although popular demand soon overcomes the possibility of picking up real bargains today. Only a few years ago the average price for a character or figural bottle was less than $4; wanted ones now go much higher.

Interest in bottles is based not only on their form but also on what they contained. This is the case with *bitters bottles*, which are being collected avidly at the moment. These were the "medicine" bottles that held concoctions (more alcohol than anything else) that were supposed to cure every human ailment. They were a legitimate way for the teetotaler to get a lift without touching "spirits." Often they were nothing more than alcohol, water, and a few herbs to give a slight laxative effect and a bitter taste. They were the cure-alls sold in the "medicine shows." Whenever some local form of prohibition put the brakes on the retailing of spirituous liquors and wines, the sale of bitters soon rose in the area. Thus they can be found all through the 1800's but their heyday was 1860 to 1900. After that the pure food laws and the general feeling of the public about "patent medicines" and the bitters frauds put a stop to them, except for a few sporadic outbursts of "tonic wines" and "medicinal bitters" in the Prohibition era.

The field for the collector is wide. Even if he contains his search to those bottles that are definitely called bitters on their labels, he will find over a thousand so marked either with a paper label or with the name impressed in the glass. The labels were used on early brands until mechanical skills in glassmaking made it possible for the bitters manufacturers to have their nostrums put up in privately marked bottles. As observed before with glass, the labels have often been lost.

You can find bitters bottles in all shapes and sizes. Characteristic are the dark amber and brown used in the later 1800's because it was thought the dark color hid any dregs that might have accumulated on the bottom. Early bottles were more likely aqua, but they can also be found in various shades of green and occasionally in blue and amethyst. They are not selected for their beauty so much as for their origin; the name of the bitters is what most collectors go by. Because the collecting of bitters bottles is relatively recent, there has not been much literature developed exclusively and comprehensively about these bottles (*see* Bibliography), but any serious collector will need some for reference to find his way around among the hundreds of kinds of bitters bottles he is apt to meet in the market. Prices are still not exorbitant for the available ones. You can get good ones from $4 to $8, but a few can run as high as $20. But when you realize that most of these have been rescued from cellar trash and dumps, even these prices seem unrealistic.

Figural bottles are those made in the shapes of animals, people, or inanimate objects. They were made as early as 1860 and were often bitters bottles, such as the famous Indian queen bottle, log cabin, fish, Washington bust, lighthouse, barrel, pig, drum, horseshoe, ear of corn, globe, and cannon, most of them made before 1880. These, an early attempt to woo the public with novel packaging, started a flood of figural bottles for all kinds of commercial products in the 1900's. Some of the popular figural bottles bought by collectors today were made as late as 1930, notably the Carry Nation and Mr. Pickwick vinegar bottles. Even today manufacturers are following up this figural bottle craze with containers for syrups or cleaning fluids that could eventually become collectors' pieces except that they are not made as carefully as the older ones. In fact, a flask containing a popular cleaning fluid currently sold in the supermarkets, with impressed patterns of George Washington and an eagle, was recently offered as old and bought at a public sale for $6.00! This stresses the necessity of knowing something about what you are buying and the ability to recognize the spurious from the real. Nevertheless, many figural bottles made today, such as for liquor at Christmas time and for perfume, are worth saving for future value as well as present interest.

Many figural bottles came in china as well as in glass, such as the Ma and Pa Carter's Ink bottles, a pair of which could run to $15 or $20. Many of the pottery bottles are imports from

France, and some are made by many of the best potteries in England and other countries. There is a French china version of the Carry Nation bottle.

These figural bottles originally contained, besides bitters, perfume, liquor, vinegar, cologne, ink, syrup, condiments, liniment, shampoo liquid, and hair tonic. What they contained is not of so much interest to the collectors as the shapes and the labels telling where, when, and by whom they were made. A bottle with an old label is always more valuable. Many of the figural bottles were pressed of clear glass and then painted to help the illusion of the figure; the paint has often worn off. Many were souvenir bottles—the milk glass bottle issued at the time of the New York World's Fair of 1939 is now worth $4.50. Most of the later bottles were made with cork stoppers, but a few had glass stoppers. Screw tops were used after 1863, when they were first made for preserve jars and salt cellars.

A sideline of figural bottles are the candy containers to which many collectors devote their interest and energy. These small figural bottles held small candies and were sold at candy stores, on trains, and at resorts. They were a 20th-century development, made from 1905 to the 1930's. Common among them are such shapes as lanterns, locomotives, suitcases, telephones, fire engines, Santa Clauses, pistols, trumpets, autos, liberty bells, airplanes, dirigibles, dogs, turkeys, and radios. Prices for these are still reasonable although they have risen with the tide of their popularity. The range now is about $4 to $7 a piece.

Figural bottle collecting is an amusing hobby. Seldom do the bottles have any claim to quality, although they show great ingenuity and, occasionally, very occasionally, intrinsic beauty.

Also in the bottle collecting field are *poison bottles*. They date from the mid-1800's, but many, especially those of the figural variety, appeared after 1900. Early ones were pressed with some kind of protuberances, spikes, knobs, etc. to make recognition immediate even in the dark. They were the effort of drug firms to prevent accidents in the home. Today, when it is easy to flick a switch for light, they are not quite so necessary, although there is no doubt that they would be a useful extra precaution even now. They come in enough variety to please the collector. Skull and crossbones were favorite modes of identification. Some bottles were skull-shaped, some had skull stoppers, or a skeleton impression. Many of the skull bottles were facetiously used for liquor in the 1920's. The snake was also used as a warning in some way on poison bottles. Some were coffin-shaped. All were dramatic warnings of what could happen if the contents were treated with too much familiarity. This kind of collection can be amusing.

Still other collectibles exist in the bottle field. Some people go in for old beer bottles with the name of the brewery imprinted upon them. Some collect all liquor bottles made before Prohibition (1920) when bottles containing spirits were imprinted, "Federal law forbids the sale or re-use of this bottle," so that they would not be used for bootleg liquor. Others go in for old soda or pop bottles, or for nursing bottles. Some people even collect the old milk bottles first made when milk ceased to be sold in bulk; when cartons entirely replace bottles for milk, our present glass milk bottles will probably turn collectibles. Miniature bottles used as samples for various liquors interest other collectors. These are fairly modern but someday they may be unique and valuable. All of these are fun collections, but as antiques are not too important.

Miscellaneous Glass Items

Insulators, those colored glass caps that were used on electric and telephone poles until fairly recently, have caught the fancy of the collectors, chiefly because of their glowing colors. Many visitors to the antiques shops do not recognize them and ponder on what they were for, as I did when I first saw a pair in a New England shop. They had been set in glass saucers but I knew they were not fairy lamps, nor could they have been used for vases because of the rounded tops unless set in some kind of stable containers. I was told by the dealer that they were used principally as paperweights or as simply bits of color in a window with other colored glass.

The majority are found in light green or aqua bottle glass, but less often they are found in more glowing colors, much as dark, rich blue, dark green, amber, and a rich amethyst that suggests Sandwich glass both in color and in the bubbly look of the glass. This is the color of the first two I saw, which now repose proudly on my window shelf. They are rare. Some clear ones have become purple by exposure to the sun like the old window glass. This happens, I believe, in the Western desert regions. Many have the name of the manufacturer impressed on them. Since they have been discovered by collectors, boys are shinnying up old poles to pick them off and digging around the poles where workers on the lines tell me they often bury these old insulators. When the word gets around that they now bring from $2 up to $5 to $7 each, there will be no more interring. A row of these in a sunny window can be quite delightful.

The same can be said for colored glass *eyecups.* They can be found in many colors, sapphire blue, dark green, peacock blue, and even red. The only thing to recommend them is their color.

Flower vases, originally part of the equipment in fine autos, are turning up on the market. They come in cut glass, pressed glass, clear and in colors. They were usually cornucopia-shaped and were held in metal brackets. They make nice wall vases today and are well worth the few dollars asked for them.

Paperweights have been collector items for years. But for the beginner today it is impossible to get the old ones if money is a factor in the buying. Consequently, many of us have had to turn our backs on the Baccarats and other French weights of the 1850's, the Sandwich, Gillinder, and Pairpont weights of the 1880's, and go looking for the late weights that may have interest if not the same artistry. There are many souvenir weights to be found, also advertising items, all dating from 1900 or later. There are also modern "sulphides," with the portraits of contemporary personages such as General Eisenhower, or Queen Elizabeth, in a silvery effect imbedded in the center of the clear glass globe. There are also many more or less contemporary paperweights in millefiori (in which small glass canes are cut transversely and set to resemble a group of many flowers). One of the most expensive and renowned American weights dates from 1905 to 1912, the Millville Rose, made by Ralph Barber, at Millville, New Jersey. Even the early copies of the Millville weight, with a single rose in pink, yellow, white, or red and showing a similar footed base with perhaps a baluster stem, sell at close to $100.

Two names that are becoming well known today to the paperweight collectors are Charles Kasiun and Paul Ysart of Scotland whose modern weights are museum pieces and when found are very expensive. A small signed Kasiun weight will cost about $125. For those who cannot afford such prices, there are other late paperweights that show real quality. Recently I was able to pick up a few in Europe, one a lovely azure blue opaque weight with gold Napoleonic bees, bought at the Baccarat factory for $10. A Venetian weight of clear glass, enclosing a single yellow rose, looks worth far more than the two dollars I paid for it. I consider them both quality pieces, with value that will increase over the years.

There are a lot of Oriental paperweights around that came into the country about twenty-five years ago. They occur in the millefiori patterns and can easily be mistaken for older ones. One way to test them is to lift them—they are not so heavy as the old weights. Most of them have rough ground flat bases; good weights have convex bottoms. The Chinese glass is apt to be a bit on the cloudy side and to the fingers of the uninitiated, the glass has a greasy or wet feel. Also the design comes close to the top of the glass. There is no reason why these cannot be added to a collection if one knows what one is getting and does not pay too much for them. They are pleasant to look at even if not tops in quality.

One of the latest items in glass to enter the ranks of the new collectibles are the *shades* for gas lights and electric lights (*see* photo section). Many were made after the turn of the century. Some are not too valuable, often of simple frosted or etched glass or in clear pressed glass patterns. But many represent the best efforts of the makers of art glass of the period. The gas shades can be recognized because they fit a larger rung, four to five inches, necessary to avoid the flame. Some of these, in the old Hobnail or Cranberry glass, make very nice shades for converted oil lamps, where the original shade has been lost or broken. But it is among the electric bulb shades that you meet some of the very fine specimens of art glass made after 1900. You can recognize these by the diameter of the base, which is usually two and a quarter inches. Most of these have come from old chandeliers and can be found singly or in the full complement of four, five and six in which they were used on a ceiling fixture. Some dealers buy the fixture just for the shades or they will keep the whole chandelier to be used in a room that will take such a dated decorative item. But the odd single shades sell well because they can be adapted for use on small electrified lamp bases, or on candlesticks, as night lights.

Among those sold in the shops are many signed shades, worth, of course, much more than the unsigned. You can still find these new antiques with the marks of Tiffany (L.S.T.), Quezal (signed with Quezal on the under rim), Steuben (with a silvery fleur-de-lis, a ribbon, and the name Steuben), and Vahlsing (marked Luster Art). Many shades put out by other companies were not marked at all. There are fine unsigned shades that resemble the work of the Durand and Imperial factories. It is said that Quezal made nothing but shades for two years.

Most of the shades are iridescent and there is much aurene either in the lining or on the outer surface. A favorite pattern is the Larson hooked feather. Mr. Charles Bassett, a collector who has given the subject much study, says Larson worked with unusual dexterity but he was not able to pass on the secrets of his skill to the Steuben workers. Durand, for whom Larson also worked, shows this hooked feather in shades and vases, and some similar shades, though unmarked, may also be Larson's work. There are also shades in orange carnival that when lit give a pleasing effect. Many unmarked shades are thought to be of foreign origin.

Keep in mind if you use an electric shade upright on a base, instead of hanging it down as it was originally used, to choose a design that will not be upside down when the shade is thus reversed. Prices for these shades fluctuate considerably, but you can be fairly sure you won't get a Tiffany for less than $25, a Quezal for $15. Unmarked shades run $2 to $8.

Another type of collectible electric shade is that of leaded glass, the same as was used for the overhead dome lights. No doubt Tiffany made many of these smaller ones, too. They were designed for the brackets of a chandelier or for wall sconces. They were usually round, about the size of a small cabbage, or trumpet-shaped, with the glass petals leaded together and overlapping. Smaller shades of brass or bronze with set-in panels of colored glass come from this same period. Many firms made them and they are called Tiffany-type. The leaded ones run $10 to $12.50 apiece.

Here and there in the shops a few pressed *tiles* of colored glass are showing up, indicating that these had a certain popularity in their day. They were probably used as borders for fancy windows. Sandwich made them. It is known that Jonathan Haley, of Rovanne, and Fostoria, Ohio, patented a method of pressing shade designs in glass tiles in the late 1880's and in 1892. How many followers he had is not easy to determine, but it might be an interesting line for the student of turn-of-the-century glass to pursue.

One glass category that belongs to this period of the last seventy years are the *souvenir pieces*. Some collectors have gone in for souvenir glass in a big way, and while it usually has no special claim to quality, it is amusing and colorful when it is partly or wholly red. A windowful of it can be very effective, especially when it is used to screen out some undesirable view.

Most of this glass was made between 1895 and 1900. It was a big output of the Pittsburgh factories that made it with the idea of reproducing a red glass for mass consumption that would be cheaper than the imported Bohemian or ruby glass so popular in the later 1800's. The glass was apt to be flashed with red, a much cheaper process than adding a copper or gold chloride to the batch before firing, which was the general procedure for producing red glass.

Wholesale houses all over the country could order this cheap red or red and clear glass for inscribing with whatever they chose as souvenirs. Retail dealers could add their own names, or that of a customer's, or a resort, such as Atlantic City, Niagara Falls, Coney Island, etc. Or sometimes it was a more personal inscription such as, *For Mother* or *Maggie to Mary and Lizzie, Asbury Park, 1905*. The inscription was done to order, etched or needle-scratched through the red flashing, while the buyer waited. Many merchants also ordered such glass pieces as giveaways for advertising or at Christmas time.

Tumblers, pitchers, goblets, mugs, vases, loving cups, toothpick holders, baskets, pin trays, hair receivers, and such small items were usually a combination of clear glass with red flashing to accent the pattern, such as the King's Crown (already mentioned under *Late Pressed Glass*), or one of the several block patterns of the imitation "cut-glass" patterns.

There was another kind of souvenir glass called *Koral*, which was opaque white with gold trimming. This could also be inscribed. It is rarer than the red and white, rare enough to excite the collectors.

While some souvenir pieces are worth buying on their own merit, they belong for the most part in fun collections especially when the more amusing inscriptions are sought.

Collecting new antique glass of any kind can be an absorbing and rewarding hobby. There is much to search for, values in many areas are reasonable—and a good many of them sure enough to rise with time to make many rather modest collections an investment.

CHAPTER 5

CHINA AND POTTERY

THOSE who collect old china are often confused by the
variety of terms used to identify it, so I would like to try
to help clear up this point before we discuss the ceramics (all
pieces made by the firing of clay) used in this country at the
turn of the century. China was the word used originally for
the fine wares imported from China to Europe, and eventually
to America, in the 1700's. It was actually porcelain, the finest
kind of china, but the word china continued to be employed
as an overall term for all kinds of household wares, both ornamental and useful. We still use it that way today. But many
authorities cringe when we speak of porcelain as china. They
prefer to keep the word china for less worthy examples of the
potter's art. Let's see what the difference really is.

Porcelain is a hard-paste ware, long known to the Chinese,
but developed in Europe in 1708 by Johann Boettger in Meissen when he happened on a deposit of kaolin clay, essential in
the making of porcelain. Petuntse was added to give it luster,

and feldspar for strength. The result was a pure white, hard, translucent ware that required only one firing, at a very high temperature of 1300 or 1400 degrees, which integrated the glaze with the base. Up to the time of the adoption of porcelain in Europe and England, china was soft-paste, made from various clays that required two firings of about 1100 degrees each, one to set the base and the second for the glaze. It was light in weight, and often of a grayish or bluish cast. You can tell it now, usually by the weight alone, or by seeing the glaze as a separate layer, should it break or chip.

There are various degrees in the softness and hardness of china, which often explains the names you find. There is a bone china made by adding bone ash to the other ingredients. It is close to true porcelain and is often called artificial porcelain. There is ironstone (or graniteware), a heavy, sturdy ware, first patented by the Mason brothers in England in 1815, to which pulverized iron slag was added for strength. Semiporcelain is an in-between ware, lighter than ironstone but not translucent or as fine as porcelain. Stoneware, from which most of the jugs and crocks for household use were made, is not pottery but a hard-paste ware given a slight glaze by the addition of salt in the firing. Bisque, parian, basalt, jasper, agateware, are all hard-paste.

Pottery, or earthenware, on the other hand, is soft-paste, usually made from local clays. As a rule you find it gray, red, tan, or brown in color, though the original color is often covered with a hard, high glaze. Delft, faïence, majolica, luster, sgraffito, and Rockingham are all soft-paste earthenware.

China was decorated in various ways, sometimes under the glaze (when the glaze was added separately), and sometimes over it. Most china was hand-decorated until transfer printing came into use in 1756. This was a method devised by Sadler and Green, potters of Liverpool, and it appeared on much of the good china of the time, even porcelain. It consisted of engraving a metal plate or a special stone (like the lithography process) and coloring it with enamels. Tissue papers were then printed from it, one for each color, and from them the designs were transferred to the china. It was a cheap process and in a modified form is still used in various ways today. Sometimes it was used in combination with hand-painting (see the discussion of late German china later in this chapter). Colors and any gold touches were baked on permanently in the firing, except in some very cheap china (the gold or the pattern is apt to wear off on some of these).

The high period of the new antiques, from 1895 to about 1915, is not truly remarkable for its production of fine American china. True, ironstone was still being made at that time both here and abroad, but it was gradually being replaced by more delicate wares such as semiporcelain and bone china. In looking over the outputs of the china factories that flourished in this country in the late 1800's, not much stands out in quality or design.

Of course there were exceptions that have left their imprints on the history of American china. In the early years of the century we were still depending upon imports made for the American trade just as we had been almost one hundred years earlier.

Among the American firms that merit mention are:

Knowles, Taylor, and Knowles, East Liverpool, Ohio
The Wheeling Pottery, Wheeling, West Virginia, trademark La Belle
Onondaga Pottery, Syracuse, New York
Mayer Brothers, Beaver Falls, Pennsylvania
Cartwright, East Liverpool, Ohio

The Potters Cooperative Company, Dresden Pottery Works,
East Liverpool, Ohio

Homer Laughlin, Newell, West Virginia (moved from East
Liverpool, Ohio, in 1897)

The American China Company, Steubenville, Ohio

Warwick China Company, Wheeling, West Virginia

New England Pottery Company, Boston, Massachusetts

Ceramic Art Company (later Lenox), Trenton, New Jersey.

These are only a few of the many factories that made china
and pottery in the United States in the later 1800's and early
1900's. Some are still operating today. Checking through a
book of china and pottery marks, one can find there over 150
names of firms and their marks. (*See* Bibliography.) Many went
in and out of business quickly, some lasting only a few years.
The centers of chinamaking were Trenton, New Jersey, East
Liverpool, Ohio, and towns in West Virginia close to Ohio,
such as Newell. Those in production around the turn of the
century turned out semiporcelain sets in tune with the taste
of the times. This semiporcelain was a lighter-weight china,
having more sturdiness than pure porcelain and less translu-
cence. You might class it as halfway between ironstone and
porcelain or even bone china (the latter is a porcelain made
first in England by the potters of the late 18th and early 19th
century by adding bone ash to hard-paste porcelain, the process usually accredited to Josiah Spode).

The general run of the semiporcelain sets in the early 1900's
had little character of design but they were "pretty," which is
really the best word for almost everything in this period. Dainty
little sprays of flowers were scattered over the surface and conventional designs were delicately scrolled. The robust designs,
the vivid colors, the Oriental elegance, and the picturesque
transfer-printed scenes and patterns were all things of the past.

Today this china is eagerly bought by those who understand the decoration and to whose taste it appeals.

One of the finest porcelain made in this period was called *American Belleek*. True Belleek, a delicate, tissue-paper-thin porcelain with a pearly luster, was first made at Fermanagh, Ireland, in 1851. It appealed to the American china-lovers to such an extent that it not only was imported in quantity, but inspired many of our factories to make an American version of it, some very fine indeed. Much of it was sold as blanks for amateurs to decorate with hand-painting. The first to make American Belleek was Ott and Brewer (Etruria Pottery of Trenton, New Jersey) in 1884. Their marks were a crescent, a crown and sword; initials O and B; or the firm name in a circle. This firm closed in 1893. They were followed in 1894 by the Cook Pottery Company, which lasted until 1900; its mark was three feathers and the word, Etruria. Others who made this American Belleek in the 1890's were the Ceramic Art Company, which used an artist's palette for a mark; the Columbian Art Company, of Trenton, New Jersey, with an M and N inside a scroll and marked Belleek; and lastly, in 1903, the Lenox Company, of Trenton, New Jersey, a name associated for many years with fine porcelain. Their marks were an artist's palette with an L, on blanks to be decorated at home, and an L in a laurel wreath, with the name below, on commercial china. When you go into a shop and ask for Belleek, meaning the Irish product, you may be shown one of the several kinds of American Belleek. If you want the original Irish china look for the old black mark—a hound, harp and tower, or a harp and crown. There is nothing wrong with the American Belleek but be sure you know what you are getting. You will probably pay more for the Irish porcelain, especially that with the old mark. After 1891 the name, Ireland, was added to it, or maybe only the words Fermanagh, Belleek Co. A cup and saucer with the old mark will cost $12 or more.

One type of fine American china made in this period deserves special mention. It is *lotus ware,* made by Knowles, Taylor, and Knowles, in East Liverpool, Ohio. Its mark—when used—was KTK, followed later by the mark of a lotus flower and the name, Lotus Ware. This was a beautifully executed type of bone china, a warm white in color, brightly glazed and showing decorations of flowers, feathers, etc., in pastel colors, with some gold. A worker from Ireland, named Joshua Poole, was brought over by the company to develop what they hoped would be an outstanding triumph in porcelain for America. The result was a dazzling white, translucent body of bone china with a velvety glaze. It resembled in grace and delicacy the bloom of a lotus flower.

The Knowles plant was destroyed by fire in 1889, but it was rebuilt the next year when a German was brought over to elaborate the designs of this ware in tune with the fussier ideas of the period. The result was a ware something like English Coalport. In this period much of the decoration was in enamel, built up or applied over the white glaze in jewel or fishnet fashion. Some figures were made. By far the most dramatic and interesting pieces were those with partial or overall applied decorations in enamel in lacy or netted effects.

Later on, two brothers, George and Will Morley, from the Doulton factories in England, took over the Knowles' color decorations and turned out dainty floral or feathery effects in soft pastel tones with a liberal addition of gold. Some transfer printing was used. Pieces of this period were exhibited at the Chicago World's Fair in 1893.

The elaborate white pieces with their applied jewellike festoons and motifs, especially the vases and bowls and other covered ornamental pieces, are easily recognizable because they are unique in American china, but the painted, decorated ware is not easy to identify unless marked. Why such fine work was left unmarked is hard to say, except that in the case of sets it was often the custom to mark only one piece, and many pieces from broken-up sets have come on the market unmarked. This version of American Belleek, in spite of its fragility, was made for use. It is found in full tea sets, cups and saucers, bowls, serving dishes, potpourri jars as well as ornamental vases and other items. Lotus ware was not made after 1897. Because of the skill and artistry involved in its making, it never went into mass production. But it belongs to the turn of the century. It is scarce, and that, plus its quality, puts it in the high-priced class of new antiques, much higher than the Belleek that inspired it. When marked, almost any piece could bring well over $100.

Without doubt, this American Belleek represents the finest in American china at the turn of the century, but there are other varieties that claim the attention of the collectors. The products of the Buffalo Pottery Company of Buffalo, New York, are meeting a demand at the moment. This factory was organized primarily to make china for the Larkin Company, a firm that many of us can remember as one of the first exponents of the direct manufacturer-to-consumer trade. One bought Larkin soap from the man at the door and got a premium or credit toward some household item—a piece of silver, or some of this Buffalo china—much like our trading stamps today. It was Elbert Hubbard (see Chapter 3) who inaugurated the merchandising schemes for his brother-in-law, Larkin. Hubbard had worked for a soap company in Chicago before he went to Buffalo to manufacture soap and become a partner in the Larkin Soap Manufacturing business. The premium method of selling soap boomed so greatly under Hubbard's direction that the company finally had to establish its own china factory.

The Buffalo Pottery Company first produced a semivitreous china, not true porcelain but not as heavy as ironstone. It was a highly acceptable ware for tea sets and dinner sets, and aside from being given as premiums for Larkin sales it was widely distributed throughout the wholesale trade. The firm was very good at under-glaze decoration, especially pieces printed in blue in the English manner. It is said that their Blue Willow pattern was equal in quality to most of the English products. Most pieces were gilt-trimmed. There were at least a dozen patterns for Larkin buyers to choose from. Aside from the Gold Band and Willow patterns, most of them were printed in dainty floral or ornamental banded designs. It was the tableware of our grandmothers acquired as a wedding gift or assembled through steady purchase of Larkin products. It was usually marked on the underside with the figure of a buffalo and the name, Buffalo Pottery. Often, the year of manufacture was added. In the case of painted designs, the artist was apt to add his name or initials.

One type of Buffalo pottery, which is more in demand than the tea and dinner sets, is *Deldare*. This is also a semiporcelain made in the 1900's. The decorations, hand-painted under a beautiful glaze, were to compete with the Royal Doulton ware from England that was flooding the American market at that time. It was originated by Lewis H. Brown, who came to Buffalo from Trenton, New Jersey, where he had learned the pottery business. His aim was to put out a line that would be associated with the decorative wares from England, and so he turned to English subjects for his designs. His first series, brought out in 1908, incorporated scenes from *The Vicar of*

Wakefield and *Cranford.* Fallowfield Hunt scenes were used
for the second series, and Richardson's *Tours of Dr. Syntax*
for the third. These were all very accurately and colorfully
executed on an olive-green ground. Deldare pieces were also
made in a series of Indian Camping Scenes and Hunting
Scenes, as well as in a historical series including Miles Standish
and Paul Jones scenes. Deldare also made commemorative
plates (*see* later in this chapter).

The making of Deldare was discontinued in 1916 and the
company turned to making hotel china for the most part. Most
of these scenic pieces are marked with the buffalo and the firm
name. Like other Buffalo pottery items, they are sometimes
dated and bear the name of the artist or his initials. Quart
jugs were a Deldare specialty, both the tall, graceful shapes
and squatty ones suggesting Dutch pottery. Prices are fairly
high. A Fallowfield Hunt plate brings about $15 or more. One
recently advertised and marked with the names of the two
artists, W. Foster and M. Tobias, was priced at $50. A Miles
Standish jug will bring $30 or more. It is a true American ware
even though it aped the English in shape and decoration. The
quality was good.

The years 1890 to 1915 were the peak period for *hand-
painted china* when the fad for this hobby swept the country.
It was a proper, ladylike accomplishment, admired in that
Victorian-influenced period. Many manufacturers here, and
in France and Germany, supplied the white blanks for china
decorating. Today, old attics and china closets are being
searched for Aunt Min's violet-decorated dresser set, for Cousin Lulu's wild-rose plates, all done freely by hand without
a pattern to go by. Some ambitious ladies painted whole
dinner sets. Needless to say, most of the painting was of a floral
nature, "pretty" rather than strongly or originally painted.

But as oddities these hand-painted pieces are coveted by collectors.

Many factories cashed in on this craze by bringing out what they called hand-painted china, which was actually decorated in their own workrooms in a different way from that used at home. Often the method was to use a transfer-printed print for the outline and touch it up or fill it in with hand-applied colors. The Doulton-Burslem factory, in England, did a great deal of this work in the 1890's. Not too long ago I happened on a dozen dinner plates so treated and they were truly beautiful. Each had a figure of a bird in its natural habitat—sparrow, parrot, robin—twelve of them, each bird different. The coloring and conception were very fine. On the back of each plate was the word, *deposé,* meaning that the pattern is registered and cannot be copied. A number of German artists were employed to do china painting in the factories, and one who signed his work A. Koch is a favorite with collectors today. He did many fruit designs on dark backgrounds.

Hand-painted china varies in price according to the quality of the work. Plates average $7.50 to $15.00 each; wall plaques, of which there were many, can go to $25. This is an area where good taste is most important, since much hand-painted china falls short in the quality of the work, although not perhaps in the china itself.

A very fine American china, made by a firm named *Pickard,* was established in Chicago in 1897. This company imported its pure white blanks from Europe. Some Pickard pieces bear the antler Wurtemburg factory imprint. The china was showy, an elegant ware sold in jewelry stores for gifts. It was often entirely encrusted with gold and in addition was beautifully decorated with floral and scenic patterns by skilled artists who signed their pieces. The mark is Pickard, within a diamond in gold.

Much fine china was imported into this country at the turn of the century. Probably the best known and most often recovered from among the things our grandmothers and mothers used is *Limoges* or *Haviland*. Haviland was made in Limoges, but not all china marked Limoges was Haviland. Limoges was a china-making center in France, near Saint-Yriex, which was the chief source of kaolin and petuntse, the clays from which porcelain is made. The first factory there was established in 1771, but during the rest of the century and the whole of the 19th century, so many factories sprang up there that it became one of the largest porcelain production centers in Europe. Many Limoges potteries later turned to large commercial production of china manufactured primarily to sell in America. But the quality was still there and the decorations continued to be delicate and well-applied. Many marks of various makers identify Limoges china, combined with the words, France, or Limoges, when it was sent over after 1891. The mark T and V is frequently found, as well as the various Haviland marks.

The story of Haviland is an interesting one. The Haviland family was long associated with china-making. The first to enter the china business were Edmund and David Haviland, New York china importers. David established his own factory in Limoges in 1842 under the name of Haviland and Company. Throughout the years many changes within the family followed, and, finally Theodore Haviland, a son of David, withdrew from the partnership, and set up in Limoges, France, his own production of what he called *La Porcelaine Theodore Haviland*. This is the Haviland that most of us have or recognize. The marks varied. The T.H. monogram, with Limoges, France, and the words, Porcelaine Mousseline, were used after 1892. By 1914 it became *Theodore Haviland*, with the Limoges, France, done in red, occasionally green. When Theodore died in 1920, his son continued the business. By 1941, the son, William David Haviland, bought out other French heirs to the name and started a business in America. The mark then became *Theodore Haviland, Made in America.*

While the various Haviland factories made other things, the chief export to this country was dinnerware. How many patterns were made is impossible to tell, but authorities have been at work tracing them and recording them. A series of books (*see* Bibliography) lists over two hundred patterns, numbering them as a guide for dealers and buyers. Many people who have the remnants of old Haviland sets now find it possible to complete them by locating pieces to match their sets, thanks to this numbering.

There is no doubt that this porcelain is worth acquiring. In spite of the fact that it was made in quantity, it retained its first fine quality and the decoration was never slipshod. It is the standard by which much fine dinnerware is judged today.

The patterns are a reflection of the tastes of the time, dainty rather than startling, with much gold used in the decoration. In fact the Haviland Wedding Ring pattern of gold banding is practically a classic and is a symbol of elegance even today.

Surprisingly enough, prices for Haviland are not too high. A full dinner set of about 100 pieces will run $200 to $250, according to pattern, but many single pieces cost less than $10. A gravy boat might cost $10, a covered dish about $15.

The marks of other French factories appeared on imported china around 1900 and later. Names like Luneville and Sarguemines, both old potteries that originally made faïence pottery (similar to majolica), turn up occasionally on good-quality semiporcelain china in late 19th-century styles of decoration.

While England was still sending over its ironstone—"thresher's china," as it was called in America—after 1891, most of the imports were of the finer semiporcelain type. Much of this semiporcelain was sold by importers located in New York City, and through the mail-order catalogs. Patterns were flowery with much gold. These, for the most part, were from factories that had kept up production of fine porcelain into the late 1880's. One was *Minton*. Cupboards in old houses, where families have been china-conscious for two or more generations, are almost sure to have some Minton, even whole dinners sets. It is beautiful, both in the texture of the bone china and in the very elegant decoration, which resembles French Sèvres; the decoration is dainty in design but has slightly bolder colors than other porcelain of its time. In fact, the Sèvres factory has some examples of early Minton in its museum. Most china importers in America numbered it among their finest wares. The mark of the later period, late 1800's to early 1900's, is a globe, sometimes showing latitude and longitude lines, with Minton across the middle.

Much *Royal Worcester* china was exported to the United States in the 1890's and early 1900's and bought by the same people who bought Minton. It was mostly bone china or semiporcelain, decorated in the same manner as much of the china of the late Victorian period, but not to be compared with the early Worcester porcelains of the periods of Dr. Wall (1751) or Flight, Barr (1793) so prized by collectors of the best English china of earlier periods. What you find in the shops today is usually from this late Victorian period and was popular in American homes from 1890 on. It is not exorbitant in price. Late plates with floral patterns can be found for $8 to $12, a decorative vase for $30. Royal Worcester is still being made today.

The *Doulton* potters made much late china that was imported into this country after 1890. It was hand-decorated porcelain and much of it was made at the Doulton-Burslem factory. What is known as Doulton-Lambeth is pottery with a tan, salt-glazed appearance like stoneware, made at another Doulton factory in Lambeth, much of which also came to America in the beginning of this century. You will find mugs, pitchers, and figures in this pottery, but it is their late decorated china, with British pictorial subjects of hunting and tavern scenes, Dickens characters, etc., that attracts the buyers. Here, as in all the late imports, there is one thing that identifies the period—the name of the country where it was made. The McKinley Tariff Act of 1891 decreed that this be added to all goods manufactured for export to America. Anything made before that time will not show the name of the country unless it was destined for sale over here after 1891. Occasionally this identification does not work. Someone traveling abroad might pick up a late piece not marked for American export and bring it in himself, but this is the exception.

Doulton still goes on, as does *Wedgwood*, always a favorite, whether made in the 1700's or now. One beautiful thing about Wedgwood is that the quality never seems to change, though forms and decorations might. Maybe experts can tell the difference between an old piece of blue Jasper and a lovely "bring-home" piece bought in London today, but only the mark will give it away. Wedgwood marks number over twenty; students can place the date of a piece fairly accurately by consulting a book showing the various Wedgwood marks and dates. My own wedding china dinner set was Wedgwood, bought in the late '20s. I can't remember the marking but I was very proud of it.

China collecting became very popular in the 1890's and among the favorites was *Crown Derby*, put out by the Crown Derby Porcelain Company in England. The mark, bearing the words Royal Crown Derby, over a crown, was adopted in 1890, with the England added later. One writer of the early 1900's, describing the output of the factory, emphasized the great quantities of tea and dinner sets made there and mentioned the use of versions of the old Japanese Imari patterns, such as were used on the early Derby of 1825–1830. This Derby was of eggshell thinness and one of the more delightful of the late imports.

Another type of late English china is an ironstone the collectors are calling *"flow blue,"* because the rich all-blue patterns show the color blurred, often running into the white background. It is not to be confused with the old flow blue (or flowing blue or flown blue) made in Staffordshire, England, from 1825 on. These early flow-blue patterns had Oriental names such as Manila, Chapoo, Kyber, Scinde, Formosa, and others. They have been bought up so thoroughly that they are now fairly rare. The scenes were done in a dark cobalt blue, which, because of the running during firing, were smudged and so vague it was almost impossible to recognize them except for the name on the back. But the late flow blue that customers in the shops are asking for is a semiporcelain made by English potters from 1880 to 1900 and after. These pieces have more decided patterns, usually small floral sprays touched up with some gold. One of the most popular patterns is Touraine, made by Alcock, of Cobridge, from 1880 to 1900. Most pieces of a dinner set can be found in it, and the price makes it a good buy for those who like this misty blue type of china. The name is included with the mark of the maker in blue on the back of the piece.

Not dissimilar to Touraine is another pattern called Waldorf, made by Boote of Burslem, around 1918. Ophir, made by Bourne and Leigh, after 1891, is also a late version of flow blue, as is Messina, made by T. F. and W. B. Moore, probably after 1891. A set that has turned up recently, made by Doulton in Burslem, is called Madras. (*See* photo section following page 116 for late flow blue plates: Waldorf, Alcock Touraine, and Doulton Madras.) Undoubtedly there are many more patterns from this period that will come to light as the demand grows. Blue has always been the choice color among collectors, which may account for the popularity of this recent flow blue. It is, however, in excellent taste and well worth collecting. Plates in these late patterns run $4.50 to $9.50 according to size. Prices are rising almost daily.

In this same period, many china manufacturers, both here and abroad, were reviving old patterns. In the 1890's, when the public was collecting in a big way, the potteries met the demand with reproduction pieces that would have been expensive and hard to find in the original version. The Indian Tree pattern, of Chinese inspiration, goes back as far as 1780. It was revived by Minton, in fine porcelain; by Doulton, after 1891, in a pattern called Heron; by Maddock, in 1914 and again in 1921; by our own Onondaga, in 1923; and by Knowles, Taylor, and Knowles, in 1925. All are similar but not exact copies. They use the basic idea of a gnarled brown tree in the center, with sprigs of double peonies in pink, and blue daisies at the sides and the base. The border is usually a Chinese fretwork in brown or blue. Colors are soft but not dull. It has become almost a perennial in dinnerware and well worth gathering up. Coalport-Spode still makes it.

The Willow pattern puzzles a lot of people. Because it has been the common household china within the memory of most of us—much of it sold in the five-and-dime stores—it does not have the esteem it deserves. But there is good Willow and poor Willow, depending upon the quality of the china on which it is printed and on the sharpness of the design. It was originally a blue and white Canton pattern, inspired by the Chinese legend of the fleeing lovers, showing the temple, the bridge, the two figures pursued by a mandarin, and the doves into which their spirits eventually turned. It was adopted by the English potters with many variations from the late 1700's on. We find old Willow in Leeds' soft-paste, and in porcelain by Minton, Spode, Worcester, and Ridgeway. From 1891 to 1924, it was revived by Maddock, Ridgeway, Sunderland, Booth, Allerton, Wedgwood and Company (the mark of an entirely different company, *not* Josiah Wedgwood and the succeeding Wedgwood companies), in ironstone and semi-porcelain, and in our own country by Knowles, Taylor, and Knowles, as well. You may also find it marked Maastricht, made in Holland. Today if you turn it upside down, you may even find it marked "Made in Japan." It has been a staple in American china closets for over fifty years.

Another confusing pattern is Onion, also of Chinese origin. It was very popular in the early 1900's, as it is today. The original Onion was Meissen, made in Germany, another blue-and-white china also found occasionally in purple. The "onion" of the name is not an onion or a bulb, but a Chinese peach or pomegranate. When copied in Europe it was called a *Zwiebel-muster,* which is German for "onion pattern." It was modified by so many manufacturers that little remained except the blue color of the floral design, which had a decidedly Chinese look. In the original, the distinguishing crossed swords of

Meissen are found on its underside. It was copied in many variations, particularly in Denmark. In England, after 1891, a pattern similar to Onion, called Danish, was brought out; another was made in earthenware, by Furnival, in 1910. Wedgwood made an Onion pattern in the same year. There was a Ridgeway earthenware version made in 1906, an Allerton in 1921. Cauldon made it in porcelain. Meissen revived it with the crossed sword mark in 1918. The Onion pattern is still imported from Europe; the best of it in newly made pieces comes from Denmark. So if it's Onion you want, go into it carefully and look for the old marks.

A pattern very popular with our grandmothers was called Tea Leaf. It was ironstone varying in quality, some more like semiporcelain, the color white and the decoration a sprig or scattered tea leaf (which some say is a strawberry leaf) of copper luster. It was made first in 1880, and reached its peak of popularity in the 1890's. By 1900 it began to disappear, being considered too "oldtimey" or old-fashioned for the homes of 1900. But it did make the turn of the century, by golly, and much of it still lies unused in family cupboards. It is now being collected. The luster sprigs and leaf shapes varied from manufacturer to manufacturer. Meakin, Furnival, Burgess, Wedgwood and Company (remember, *not* Josiah Wedgwood), and other English potters made it. In our own country, Mayer Brothers, of Beaver Falls, Pennsylvania, and Cartwright, of East Liverpool, Ohio, each brought out a Tea Leaf china. It is getting scarce but is still not exorbitantly priced. Plates run up to $5 or $6. This is one instance where the first wave of collecting fervor has worn off and prices aren't soaring for the moment. But if you like it don't stop buying it. It's good china and worth collecting.

At the turn of the century, Germany ranked second to England as the largest china-producing country of the world. Although many of the old factories had ceased to exist, there were many newcomers scattered throughout Germany and Austria. By far the greater number were in Prussia, but many more were located in Saxony and Bavaria. And they all had their eyes on us in America, as customers. In a book by W. F. Jervis, published in 1911, it is stated that imports for 1909 from the German factories amounted to over $18,000,000, a lot of money for that time, and that the shares in some of the German houses were paying as much as 18 percent dividends. This will give some idea of the tremendous scope of their business, most of which was in the United States. German importers in New York registered the marks of their German and Austrian manufacturers, often adding their own names or sometimes adopting an entirely new mark. Charles Ahrenhardt, one well-known mark, for instance, is the name of an importer, not of a china. There are several books on German and Austrian factory marks that will help the collector to find out what he has. (*See* Bibliography.)

There is still much of this late German china around, and right now it is getting the concentrated attention of collectors. The shelves of the shops are full of it—or wish they were, because it brings good prices. It was considered a semiluxury in its time, as the quality was generally good, some of it comparable to the French Limoges. It was sold in jewelry stores as gift items. Most of it is found in single pieces. It was not primarily dinnerware. Chocolate sets were a favorite; a tall pot and six tall cups and saucers made up a set. Following are some of the names you will meet if you set out on the search for late German and Austrian china:

Royal Bayreuth. Bayreuth was the 18th-century center for several manufacturers of faïence (glazed pottery like majolica) and had its workshops where their artists painted Meissen porcelain. But it is the later products of one Bayreuth factory that make the present market in this china. Considering that the plant closed in 1905, there is a lot of this china around. By far the most characteristic are the novelty items. Most of the red tomato pieces (*see* photo section for examples), creamers, sugar bowls, and mustard pots; the lobster dishes; the devil and card pieces—often souvenir items, such as a creamer with playing-card sides and a red devil for a handle; small pitchers shaped like animals, cats, dogs, moose, pigs, cows, bears, poodles, are all Bayreuth pieces. This firm also made the Sunbonnet Babies pieces, about which more later. Many were cheap enough to be sold in the five-and-dime stores, but they bring fancy prices now. There were other things with the Bayreuth name. A pattern called Rose Tapestry, which looks just like its name, with an all-over ground in a woven effect on which is a design of roses, is a popular item in the shops. A plate in this pattern could cost as much as $25. Bayreuth pieces also show pleasant scenes in soft colors. The Bayreuth blue mark after 1891 had the word Bavaria added to it. The founding date of the factory (1784) was incorporated in the mark, which fact leads many people into thinking wrongly that it is the date of manufacture of the particular piece.

R. S. Prussia is the mark and the trade word for the Reinhold Schlegemilch firm, which sent imports to this country up to 1918, when War World I stopped the flow of German china. It was made in Suhl, and its mark is a wreath enclosing the letters R S, with Prussia beneath them. After 1891, the word Germany was substituted for Prussia. Another mark of this firm bears the words Tillewitz, Germany. It was china of high distinction and refinement, comparable to the Limoges of the period. That which shows the so-called "red mark," a red star above the green wreath, is supposedly of better quality than pieces without it; it is more desirable and much more expensive.

Decorations were hand-painted floral motifs, particularly red and pink roses and poppies. German artists worked in their own homes to put out a commercial product that would compete with the hand-painted wares so popular at the time in America. Sometimes the initials or the name of the artist was added. This china has zoomed in price ever since collectors discovered, only a few years ago, that it was a ware to which nobody had paid much attention but which could be mentioned in the same breath as the best French china. Today a cracker jar would run to $25, a large bowl the same, a plate as high as $12.50. It was imported among other German china by Butler Brothers, a wholesale firm that supplied all kinds of articles for retail stores.

Royal Bonn came from an old factory established in Bonn, Germany, by Clemens August in 1755. There is also an old Bonn mark of a later date bearing the name of F. A. Mehlan. The mark is an elaborate one bearing the initials F M, within a medallion that looks like folded drapery with a crown above it. The founding date of 1755 is incorporated with it, and, like the date on Bayreuth, this is apt to be misinterpreted as the date of manufacture. Of course, any Bonn that came into the United States after 1891 bears the imprint, Germany. Bonn is of good quality and, like much of the other German china, was hand-painted, with roses predominating and the addition of much gold. The usual items appeared in Royal Bonn—vases, cracker jars, trays, and bowls. But one thing that we particularly associate with it are the fancy little mantle clocks of rococo design (*see* Chapter 3) that were fitted with Ansonia works in this country. A clock of this kind, marked Bonn, would bring about $50.

Rudolstadt is another name found in the ads of the antique dealers and considered a choice item. Rudolstadt, another old factory established in Volstedt in the 18th century, moved to Schwartzburg at a later date. Its mark incorporates a hay fork, which was part of the coat of arms of that city. Later, two hay forks crossed were used to imitate the marks of Dresden. The last mark, very similar to that of Royal Bonn, used the initials R W below a crown, and the added word, Germany. Some of the pieces resembled Dresden but more readily followed the style then current—hand-painted flowers on a cream background with gold decor. Prices compare with other German china of the period. A marked portrait plate is quoted at $15.

Teplitz, a decorative pottery found mostly in very elaborate vases, was a commercial product of the later Victorian era, and not in line with the products that came from Germany shortly after. It is grouped with these late-comers, however, and finds many customers. Sometimes the word Wien (Vienna) was added to the mark—a rose over the monogram—sometimes Bohemia. Vases run up to $35 a piece.

Royal Vienna was originally made by Du Paquier in 1716, who was aided by some workmen from the Meissen works. It equaled the Meissen porcelain in brilliance of color and technique. The original ware was made only until 1864. Later Austrian and German factories reproduced it, even to using the old "bee hive" mark that distinguished the old china. You will see Royal Vienna of the late period advertised today with the "bee hive" marking. The old Royal Vienna pieces, some decorated by famous artists such as Angelica Kaufmann, will run close to $100. The late pieces called Royal Vienna, even those made by other factories, are also high in price. A vase will bring about $30.

Karlsbad was the center of much fine china-making. (*See*

photo section for examples of Karlsbad ware.) Various marks
bearing the word Karlsbad or Vienna are to be found, sometimes with the initials of the makers or importers, such as
H and G (Hamburger and Company), C.D. (C. L. Dwenger),
the shield and lion of Bawo and Dotter, New York importers
(who also used the double-onion mark under the Queen's
rose), the Silesian mark with crossed swords, crown and armor
of S.W. and Company (Strobel Wilkins and Company, importers). The Pirkenhammer works under Fischer and Meig,
near Karlsbad, made china for America after 1890. Its marks
vary from simple initials, F and M, to crossed mallets alone
or in a shield. Philip Rosenthal, of Selb, was also a producer
of fine china from 1879 on. The mark is Rosenthal beneath
the roses and a crown or the initials R and C in a cross under
a crown.

And of course there is *Dresden,* a great favorite with our
grandmothers for fine decorative porcelain and tableware.
What was imported after 1891 was what dealers call—or should
call—*Late Dresden.* These late pieces will bear the name of
Dresden or Germany, even though they carry the crossed
swords of the old marking. Though this late version of Dresden
cannot compare with the original Meissen, the first porcelain
made in Europe, it has much to recommend it. Much of it
was copied from the early pieces decorated by inspired artists,
some made over old molds. It is easily recognizable. Tableware was usually decorated with dainty all-over patterns of
fine flowers. An occasional cup and saucer will show panels
painted with court scenes, a careful reproduction of the work
found on early pieces. There is also a "spaghetti" ware—dishes
and bowls bordered in thin lattice or basket effect. Lamps,
supported by cherubs and showing many raised rosebuds and
much gold, were late Dresden. It was romantic china, and

even though a late attempt to carry on the Meissen tradition, it was a luxury item and well worth cherishing now that Dresden and its factories have gone behind the Russian Iron Curtain. A Dresden plate will cost about $12 to $15, a three-piece tea set about $100.

Some very creditable reproductions of old Dresden figures were put out by C. G. Schierholz and Son, of Plauen, Thuringia, and were bought for wedding presents in America. I can remember a pair of these elegant figures, a courtier and his lady, seated in identical Louis XVI chairs, drinking tea. The figures occupied opposite ends of our piano for years, and, I am sure, inspired me at practice time when I was a child. One sad day, they were broken while the maid was dusting. The pieces were buried in the trash can, but unearthed by my father and brought back to the house to be held for future mending. But they never got mended. They were thrown out again during a housecleaning. Now that I have discovered that they were not real Dresden, I do not miss them so acutely. (Schierholz also made china in the Dresden manner, painted by hand, with no transfers or foundation printing being used.)

Other European countries kept the imports rolling in during the late 90's and early 1900's. One variety is *Herend*, a hard-paste porcelain from the Moritz Fischer pottery in Hungary. Its marks were Herend, M F, or a crown over a coat of arms in blue enamel over the glaze. It holds its own with fine porcelains like Minton and Dresden with the same general characteristics.

From Denmark came *Royal Copenhagen*. Most of it was in the Onion tradition, with blue under-glaze decoration. Some pieces had scenes and figures, especially the wall plaques—large plates showing pictorial subjects—that were popular in this period. The characteristic marks for Copenhagen are the three wavy lines alone, or in combination with a crown, or circle, enclosing the name. The meaning of these lines is interesting. They are a picturesque symbol of the three straits, the Sound, the Great Belt, and the Little Belt, which separate three mean sections of Denmark: the islands of Zealand and Fyn, and Jutland peninsula. The initials B and G signify the firm of Bing and Grondahl, best known for their famous Christmas plates (*see* photo section). One of their marks is a three-turreted castle, the initials B & G, and the words, Danish China Works. It is what I would call moderately priced in this day of high prices, a teapot costing perhaps $25, a small plate $5 to $6.

Bing and Grondahl were the authors of the first of the famous Christmas plates made in 1895. In friendly competition, plates marked Royal Copenhagen were produced in 1908. Both of these are sought by collectors who try to assemble as many years as possible, as the year appears on each plate. At first only 500 were made each year and the models were then destroyed. They are of under-glaze decorated porcelain, the translucent glaze giving the blue painting underneath a soft, appealing look. Every year the specific plate is different, but it always is of some subject that emphasizes the Christmas scene, with a Danish feeling. A contest among artists or members of the potteries is held each year to get the best picture for reproduction. Many famous names in the Danish art world, such as Dahl Jensen, Margrethe Hayldahl, and Ove Larsen, have been represented on these plates. Although the plates were usually seven inches in diameter, every five years the Bing and Grondahl firm makes a double size that they call a jubilee plate. Originally the word *Jul,* which is Danish for Christmas, was used on these plates, although they were often inscribed in other languages as well. Now they bear only the date with no inscription at all. There was always a border on the Copenhagen plates so you can recognize these easily.

The prices depend upon the popularity of the particular design and on the rarity. A Bing and Grondahl 1895 plate may cost $800, a 1949 plate $30. Naturally there are not many complete sets in collections, but that is always the aim of a collector. The wise ones now buy one each year as they are produced, and keep on trying to pick up the early ones.

Some china also came from the Orient in this era, notably a cheap Japanese ware called *Noritake*. These huge potteries put out a tremendous amount of china for export—and still do. What collectors look for are pieces to complete the sets of Noritake that used to be given out as premiums by the Larkin Soap Company. The most sought-after pattern is Azalea, a very dainty flower pattern in natural colors. Though not Oriental in feeling, it shows in the painting the fine touch of the Japanese artist. Noritake is still a good investment for the money, many pieces running less than $5.

Finer china from Japan also came into this country at the turn of the century. One was a late version of *Satsuma*, made in Japan over three hundred years ago. The late version, however, was mass produced and is not to be compared with the early. It has a certain value for those who like the Oriental feeling in their china. This is not to be confused with an English pattern called Satsuma that was made about 1879. The late Satsuma ware is not cheap but it is not inordinately high-priced. A small bowl might cost about $35.

There is no doubt that pieces marked Japan are becoming more popular at present. People used to look down their noses at anything made in Japan because it usually meant a cheap version of other American or European goods, but this idea is changing. Even the cheap souvenir Japanese pieces sold at resorts have become acceptable among some collectors. One variety marked *Nippon-Handpainted* compares very favorably with all the other hand-painted pieces that came in about 1900 from the continent. It is a fine, thin grade of porcelain with decorations that are rich looking but not gaudy. It often shows encrusting of gold judiciously employed. It is worth more than a passing glance. Much of it appears in small pieces, powder boxes, pin trays, and other bureau pieces. It is one of the best buys on the market at today's prices. A powder box might cost but $5, and a set of paper-thin cups and saucers daintily decorated with birds and flowers sells for only $2 a piece.

China, too, sent over pieces designed for the American trade in the early 1900's. Much blue Canton (now called *Late Canton*) came over then. It was similar to the early Canton brought over by our sailing ships in the 1800's, but it has not, of course, the same quality, and patterns only dimly resemble the old ones; nor does it command the same prices. Plates that could have been picked up a few years ago for $2 or $3 are now selling for $7 to $10. China continued to make this ware and export it until the Bamboo Curtain came down over the Chinese mainland. Anything Chinese we get now comes from Hong Kong or Formosa.

All those lovely little pieces we used to get in the Oriental shops or in Chinatown at very reasonable prices—the nut cups, small serving dishes, rice bowls, handleless tea cups and plates, with colored lining of Chinese pink, turquoise, or Chinese red —have disappeared. I remember I used to frequent the shops in Chinatown and was considered "way out" then when I used these pieces on my table. I was not particularly careful with them. But now I cherish the few that are left and treat them with great respect. In line with these were those very colorful paper panels, printed with Chinese figures and colored so

Two dolls by Schoenhut, together with clown and mule from Humpty-Dumpty circus; a complete Schoenhut circus had 20 or more figures.

Set of 1892 Brownies, designed by Palmer Cox. The figures were cut
from printed muslin sheets, sewn together, and stuffed with cotton.

Turn-of-the-century exploding toys:
Cap pistols and package of caps.
Trick book using roll of caps.
Pistol that sets a top spinning.
Pistol that snaps a ball into cup.
Rifle shape, called a "little gun."

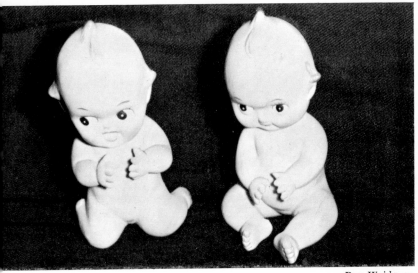

ewpie figures made of bisque, designed by Kestner firm of Germany.

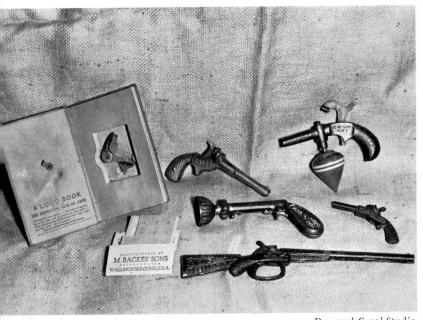

Turn-of-the-century table lamp with
shade of the popular Carnival glass.
The fixture of this lamp is modern

Dan Weidener

Dan Weidener

Items of Carnival glass, from left to right: marigold-color vase,
purple bowl, kitten-and-mouse plate, pitcher in blackberry pattern

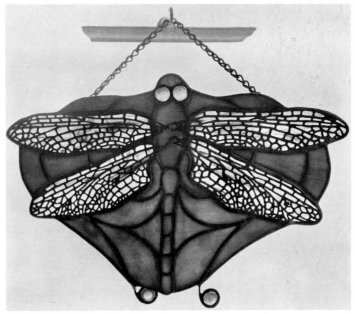

Philadelphia Inquirer
Tiffany transparency of leaded glass, hung at a window.

Dan Weidener
ariety of electric light shades includes Tiffany-type leaded glass.

Fish set of Austrian Carlsbad porcelain had a 30-inch platter, 6 plates, and sauce boat, each hand-painted with a different fish.

English porcelain in late flow blue patterns: Waldorf plate, platter by Doulton in Madras pattern, and Touraine plate by Alcock (right).

Dan Weidener

Quimper pottery, around 1910.

Dan Weidener

Royal Copenhagen Christmas plate, left, and two by Bing and Grondhal. These delicate Danish porcelain pieces are still being produced, and present a different scene for every Christmas season.

The Gibson Girl "contemplates the cloister." Gibson Girl plates, depicting events in the life of the famous lady created by popular artist Charles Dana Gibson, were made by Royal Doulton of England.

Royal Bayreuth sugar and creamer set in bright red tomato shape.

An early Rockwood vase
in vellum with an 1895
marking.

Cut and engraved bottle, made by Corning around 1890, was ordered by a New York banker for his niece, Ellen Rogers.

Tiffany table
lamp, signed.

Dan Weidener

Dan Weidener

Examples of cut glass are bowl in pinwheel pattern, bowl
in pineapple design, toothpick holder, and knife rest.

A variety of souvenir spoons, foreign and domestic, dating from 1890 o

se exquisite porcelain birds created by Dorothy Doughty, entitled
len-Crowned Kinglets in Noble Pine, recently sold at auction for $2100.

Dan Weidener

Umbrella stand in the "ball-and
stick" style, made around 189[...]

Dan Weidene[...]

A country-store pipe holder.

Lady's reclining rocking chair in the popular Bentwood style.

In country stores at the turn of the century, candy was scooped from
large containers with these glass mugs and sold for so much per cup

Country-store items: brass scoops, iron string-holder, coffee mill

lavishly with Chinese colors and much gold. Artists used them for decorative effects. For years I have had one panel about 10 by 14 inches knocking around under glass and passe-partouted with gummed tape. Just a few weeks ago I woke up and took it to a good shop and had it appropriately framed. It is the nicest wall piece I have, and I'll never get another like it.

One Chinese pattern that is enjoying great popularity at the moment is *Rose Medallion*. It was a favorite in the cupboards of the early 1900's. The pattern is a very old one in the history of Chinese Canton. Its appeal is its coloring, alternating medallions of figures, pink flowers, birds, and butterflies on a light green or white background. The flowers look more like peonies than roses, however. Smaller pieces showed four medallions, larger pieces six.

There seems to be some mystery about its origin, but the general agreement is that it was a variety of Canton made in the huge china center of King-te-chin and was originally called Mandarin china. While called porcelain, it was not as transparent as true porcelain. It is supposed to have been designed for the early China export trade and so made in shapes that would appeal more to the Westerners than to Orientals—flat plates, cups with handles, and so on.

It is hard to pinpoint the date when Rose Medallion first came into this country. Authorities state that after the War of 1812, a china called Mandarin, or Medallion, was brought in. But much more of it—probably what we are now calling Late Rose Medallion—was imported after 1862. As late as 1912, a consumer report stressed that Chinese porcelain exports had reached a peak around the world, with the United States bringing in the largest percentage.

There are supposed to be ways that you can distinguish

between the early and late examples of this china. Those who have studied them both will tell you that the early is thinner, not as heavy as the late variety, that if you look on the back you will find the early pieces rougher, and that you will find more gold in the early pieces with traces of it in the dark hair of the figures. Unfortunately neither are often marked except occasionally with the Chinese characters of the Ch'ing reign.

When there are no medallions, or reserves as they are called, just an all-over pattern of the colored flowers, butterflies, etc., this china is called *Rose Canton*. Both patterns are desirable. There is one kind of Rose Medallion that brings it definitely into the category of turn-of-the-century antiques, a ware made by Haviland and marked H and Company. It is thought that Haviland may have made only the blanks, which were decorated elsewhere. There is also a modern Rose Medallion, an out-and-out reproduction now being sold in the gift shops. Prices for the better pieces you would want to own are fairly high. Plates run about $10 and $15, a set of teapot and two cups and saucers in a basket container, $35.

Holland sent over a great deal of export china in the early years of the century. We have spoken of the Onion pattern, still going strong, but there is another popular ware that does not stay long on the shelves of the antiques shops—*Blue Delft*. Delft was originally produced in the town of Delft, Holland, in the 17th century. It was an earthenware given a tin glaze, the same process used in majolica and faïence, of which more later. But the Blue Delft that we are considering here was imported in the 1900's. It was often souvenir china, brought home by tourists in Holland at that time. It is quite charming, with characteristic Dutch scenes with windmills, ships, and children at play. Many people, particularly those who like blue, love it in any form, from a pair of small salt and pepper shakers shaped like windmills to a huge wall plaque. Pieces are not exactly cheap, but they are not impossible. A good plate will sell for about $10, a wall plaque for $30, unusual little trinket boxes about $10 or $12.

One of the largest china factories in Holland was at Maastricht. Ware from this plant was a regular import early in the 1900's. It is marked with the name of the town. Because so many British workers were employed there, the result was a china with an English look and could easily be mistaken for English wares that found their way to this country at that time. Some Willow pattern and flow blue are often found marked Maastricht. Transfer patterns showing Chinese scenes of temples, birds, and Oriental figures (called *chinoiserie*) were given the names of Pajong or Hong Kong. It was colorful, often printed in tan and black, but just as often in blue with red, green, and black decorations. The ware is not expensive but has enough quality to be a good buy. A Pajong bowl seven and a half inches in diameter could run $7 to $10. A small flow-blue bowl could go for about $4.

Italy was not so generous in supplying our market with china at the turn of the century as were the other countries. Pieces of Italian majolica found their way to America then, but the most outstanding china found in the better shops today is *Capo-di-Monte*. This lovely hard-paste white porcelain was made as early as 1740, but over the years it was copied in Germany, France, and Italy, providing us with many pieces of that name which we now buy. The Capo-di-Monte type keeps the old marking of an N and a crown. The firm of Ginori, long associated with Capo-di-Monte, still imports it. It is a lovely ware, even the newer versions, often elaborately decorated and well worth the high prices asked for it, whether old or what some call "fakes." Figures in this china are quite enchanting; an orchestra of dwarfs with musical instruments could bring as high as $360. A tea set brought in before World War II has been found priced at $58.

Pottery

Some earthenware became popular here in the 19th century and early 1900's and is well worth collecting today.

Majolica is fine pottery. Much of it was made in American factories as early as 1870, and its manufacture continued into the 1900's. What we made and what came in from England (1850–1900) might be called a cousin of the older majolica of Spain and the faïence of Italy and France. It differs from the old majolica in the glaze; older Spanish, Italian, and French faïence and the Dutch Delft, employed an opaque white tin glaze to cover the gray clay base before the vitrified colors were used for the decoration. Later, lead was employed in the glaze because it was cheaper and gave more brilliance to the colors applied under the transparent glaze. Some writers on the subject go as far as to say that American majolica, because it uses this lead glaze is *not* true majolica. However, we do not seem to have a better word for it, and most dealers and collectors call it that.

In England, many well-known potters made it, including Wedgwood and Minton. In this country it was not considered very fine ware. In fact, the Etruscan ware, of the Griffin, Smith and Hill Company of Phoenixville, Pennsylvania, which operated from 1880 to 1892, was given away with baking powder. Today, however, all 19th-century majolica, both American and foreign, is the concern of dedicated collectors, especially when marked. Not much of it is signed, however. That from the pottery of Griffin, Smith and Hill usually shows a monogram or the words, Etruscan Majolica. The Bennett firm of Baltimore, formerly the Chesapeake Pottery Company, made majolica that was signed Clifton on the bottom of all pieces up to 1882, and Avalon and Calvertine later on. Other pieces from other factories often show nothing but broad brush marks, impossible to decipher.

The leaf dish, usually a begonia leaf, is typical of American majolica; so are the sunflower syrup pitcher and the ear-of-corn jug. But since the English made similar pieces, these cannot always be identified as American. One pattern, Shell and Seaweed, is perhaps the most favored—and high-priced—pattern in Etruscan. A characteristic of late majolica is the colored lining, usually a shade of pinkish-lavender, or a blue, pink, or red. Etruscan pieces always show a pink lining. This is most effective in open pieces such as pitchers and decorative pieces. Animals were used extensively in the designing. Quite often you will come upon a fish pitcher or a parrot jug or perhaps a frog tobacco jar, all brilliantly and realistically colored under the glossy surface. Majolica prices are high. A sardine dish with a cover showing a fish as a knob or finial will bring about $24. A Shell and Seaweed cup and saucer could be worth $45, but a common leaf dish, marked Etruscan, might run only to $10. Marked American pieces seem to be preferred to English. Every once in a while a French piece such as a "mouth-pouring" pitcher (in the form of a bird or animal where the liquid is poured from the mouth as a spout), or a lattice-work bordered plate will turn up in the market, but these pieces are usually earlier than 1900. They may be marked Luneville, Palissy, Sarreguemines, or Gien. Sarreguemines is still in production. Majolica also came from Germany and many of the German potteries continued to make it until World War I, which all goes to show that majolica was not exclusively a Victorian product. If you stick to marked pieces you cannot go wrong on dating them.

One style of earthenware that is just coming to the attention of the antiques shops is a French importation of about 1900 to 1921. It is *Quimper* (pronounced kam-pair), made by Henry Quimper of Finistère, France, and is marked boldly with the name of the maker. It was very popular about the time that people were beginning to appreciate the charms of peasant china and linen for informal use. It usually shows appealing figures in Breton costume, bright-colored on grounds of white, cream, yellow, or occasionally other colors. As a change from the dainty dinnerware of the period, people welcomed this sturdy tableware on the amusing side. There must be plenty of it still around, probably still in hiding or in use, but it is being dug out by the dealers, and for this reason is well worth pursuing as a new antique. It was not expensive originally when it was sold in the department stores, but it won't be long before it falls in with the upward trend of prices. Even now prices run from $5 to $10 for a piece. A sugar and creamer will cost about $12, a whole tea set $45 or $50. You can find Quimper not only in table pieces, but in such things as inkwells, candlesticks, knife rests, etc. (*See* photo section.)

A late variety of American pottery that is becoming a popular collectible is *Dedham*. It was made in Dedham, Massachusetts, by the Chelsea Pottery Company, a firm known for its tiles. The company was established in 1872, but moved to Dedham in 1895. There they made their attractive earthenware, sometimes called crackleware because of the spiderweb effect of blue in the glaze. It was made in many bordered patterns of which the rabbit is the most outstanding motif. You can find butterflies, chickens, elephants, lions, polar bears, owls, lobsters, swans, turtles, crabs, dolphins, ducks, and other animal figures as well as flowers and fruits such as iris, azalea, water lilies, grapes, and horse chestnuts. The mark for this pottery made at Dedham (1895–1943) is the form of a rabbit, a stylized, foreshortened figure for the earlier pieces and a more realistic rabbit for the later pieces. The name Dedham, stamped in blue with the rabbit, was used in 1897; the word Registered was used with the rabbit mark from 1929 to 1943. It is a colorful ware and there is enough available in a variety of designs to attract collectors. Prices are relatively low. Plates run $8 to $15, cups and saucers about the same. A large platter could cost as much as $30.

Of all the pottery made at the turn of the century, Art Nouveau has become the thing to buy. This American-made pottery followed the trend of the Art Nouveau movement (*see* Chapter 3). Treatment of forms was natural and flowing in line. Decorations were mostly floral, with sinuous stems, soft outlines, and watery backgrounds. It was something new for America. The first Art Nouveau pottery to appear, which more or less set the trend here, was *Rookwood,* admittedly one of the world's finest examples of art pottery.

Rookwood was originated by Mrs. Maria Longworth Storer. It was named after her father's country estate, near Cincinnati, Ohio. Its development was the culmination of many years of work on her part and that of some art-conscious ladies of Cincinnati, who had become interested in the fashionable pursuit of hand-painting on china in the 1870's. Many were art students and all were serious. Their pieces were exhibited at several expositions and received complimentary notices. Two of the group, Mrs. Storer and a Miss Mary McLaughlin, went on to develop what they hoped would be a distinctive Ohio pottery. With family funds, they helped to erect two of the largest kilns ever used in this country, and experimented with Ohio clays. In 1898, Mary McLaughlin perfected a hard porcelain that she called Losanti ware, which was first exhibited at the Paris Exposition of 1901. After this she retired, but Mrs. Storer kept on with pottery and really established art pottery in this country. Her first kiln was set up in an abandoned schoolhouse that her father bought for her and made into a pottery. It was here that she began working on what she later called Rookwood. It was uphill work and probably would have failed if it had not been for her father's financial help. She did her own decorating in the first few years and at first produced commercial china, breakfast and dinner sets, decorative pieces, plaques, vases, and umbrella stands. She had the help of the sons of Joseph Bailey, with whom she had worked at the old pottery where she first experimented with ceramics. In 1883, she took in William Watts Taylor as manager, to put the pottery on a paying basis. Mr. Taylor controlled the business until his death in 1913.

During the early years, Mrs. Storer was experimenting with her under-glaze colors that finally came to a culmination in the elegant jardinieres, vases, plaques, and other decorative pieces that we know now as Rookwood. They won a gold medal at the Paris Exposition in 1889. By that time her pottery was becoming internationally famous and was putting America high on the list of outstanding potters in the world. Rookwood was universally imitated, especially after the Chicago Exposition of 1893.

There are several types of Rookwood. Classified by Edwin Barber in his *Pottery and Porcelain of the United States,* they are: first, cameo ware, shell-tinted with a beautiful pink shading into white under a high glaze; next, a dull finished creamy ware called vellum, soft to the touch, with an unglazed appearance (*see* photo section for a vellum vase); then, the rich, glazed Rookwood faïence, with blended colors under the heavy transparent colored glaze. However, other authorities classify this pottery differently: the standard Rookwood, brilliantly glazed in tones of yellow, red, and brown with luxuriant-looking flowers; the sea-green Rookwood, with a limpid effect of color and lighting under water in which designs were often fish as well as flowers; iris Rookwood, a type with an exceptionally mellow appearance; mat glaze, made at the beginning of the 20th century and known variously as mat painted, with colors suggesting flowing enamels, incised mat, with designs cut into the pottery usually in one color, and modeled mat glaze. About 1904, at the St. Louis Exposition, Rookwood came out with a vellum finish without luster but really treated with a glintless glaze. There was also a period after 1900 when a metal—bronze or silver—was applied to pieces by electrolysis in such a way that the metal seemed part of the whole design envisaged by the artist.

The distinction of Rookwood depended not alone upon its composition and coloring but upon its designs. No two pieces were alike, every piece was the expression of the decorator's individual artistic feeling. Mrs. Storer employed many painters from the art schools, particularly the Cincinnati Art Academy, and many well-known artists of the period designed Rookwood pieces. This accounts for the great variety to be found in this ware. Because its creator established a truly American type of pottery, using native clay, with no mechanical aid or help from established styles of foreign countries, each piece expressed a fresh New-World flavor.

Fortunately for lovers of this fine-art pottery, Rookwood is well marked. The RP monogram stamps it immediately. But other marks were used at other times. Early ones show the name and often the date. A unique marking, from 1886 to

1900, was to add a flame for each year to the monogram. Later, a Roman numeral was used for the year. Initials of the artist or his cipher were often added to the mark. Thus, it is not hard to place a piece of Rookwood in time or by the designer. A letter on the bottom of the piece might signify the type of clay used, C for cream, R for red, W for white, S for sage green, Y for yellow, O for olive, and G for ginger color. Sometimes letters indicated size.

Rookwood was never cheap; it was always a connoisseur's pottery, and the quality of the work demanded high prices at the time. Then, an especially well-executed vase could bring as much as $200. Today, vases will run around $25 to $27.50; a humidor will cost about $30 and a teapot, $50. The pieces most desired by collectors are those made in the 1880 to 1900 period.

Naturally, anything as successful as Rookwood would have resulted in a number of imitators, and today this related pottery is also being gathered up by collectors interested in this late period of production. Among the most outstanding was a pottery in Steubenville, Ohio, run by three men, W. A. Long, W. H. Hunter, and Alfred Daly. They put out a fine-art pottery that they called Lonhuda, coined from the first syllables of their names. This plant was purchased in 1896 by S. A. *Weller,* of Zanesville, Ohio. Mr. Long remained in Weller's employ. The ware was rechristened Louwelsa. It has a great resemblance to Rookwood in its glaze and rich coloring. Weller also produced some large pieces such as jardinieres with pedestals painted to resemble Rookwood, but bolder and broader in treatment. He often employed scenes from classics such as *Ivanhoe* and other books read at the time. This he called Dickensware. Sicard, another of his pottery types, was one made by two Frenchmen, Jacques Sicard and Henri Gellie.

It was a very fine ware that looked like glass with a metallic luster, and showed floral and conventional designs on a dark background of green, brown, or purple. Vases, plaques, candy dishes, jewel boxes, umbrella stands, lamps, and candlesticks were made by Sicard. It was sold by Tiffany in New York. When Sicard went back to France, the pottery signed with his name was discontinued. Weller pieces are usually signed with the name, Weller, and the name of the ware—Dickens-Weller; Dickensware-Weller; L.D.T., the monogram for Turada; Sicard and Louwelsa.

Another pottery similar to Rookwood is *Roseville,* which was made by the Roseville Pottery Company of Zanesville, Ohio. This, too, is now coming on the market along with Rookwood and Weller. Once, not too long ago, it went at sales for as little as ten cents, as something simply old-fashioned, but today it is taking on new stature. Roseville got some exquisite effects in slip-painted pieces (decorated with a thin contrasting clay mixture, like icing on a cake), and in *sang de boeuf* (ox blood), the ancient Chinese method of decoration, whereby a red glaze was allowed to run or slip to show a lighter color underneath. Roseville also made many carved pieces with Greek designs. Its pottery called Mara was made to rival Weller's Sicard. The Roseville pieces, mostly decorative bowls and vases, now bring close to what Weller and Rookwood do in prices, and these will continue to rise as popularity and recognition grows.

Many other firms went into the production of these art wares in the late 1890's and early 1900's. The Grueby Faïence Company of Boston, put out a lovely soft green glazed ware in mat (flat) finish with simple decorations. Another green mat ware, called Teco, was made by the Gates Potteries of Chicago. The Sophie Newcombe Memorial College, in New Orleans, opened a small pottery in 1895, and brought out a charming unglazed art ware in soft grays, and neutral greens with floral subjects. Mrs. Adelaide Alsop Robineau, of Syracuse, New York, originated some fine art pieces of both earthenware and porcelain comparable to the best French pieces. Much of this new pottery was exhibited at the St. Louis Exposition in 1904. Pieces of Louis Tiffany's *favrile* pottery were also shown there. Undoubtedly many of these will be showing up in the market, but unless they are marked, it will take time and study to authenticate them. Unfortunately not much has been written on these late producers of art ware, and so the amateur will have to go on looking, comparing, and buying what his fancy dictates.

Many china novelties cropped up in this late period. Many of us can even remember the old plate rail that ran around the wall, close to the ceiling, in most correct dining rooms. This was the housewife's way of showing off her good one-of-a-kind pieces that she could not use on her table. Plates arranged this way on a rail served as decoration, and did not take up the room they would have required on cupboard shelves. From this plate rail come many items that antiques collectors look for today.

Take the *Gibson Girl plates,* for instance. This aristocratic glamor girl was created by Charles Dana Gibson, for the old magazine, *Life,* and other periodicals adopted her. It is said that the artist often used as model his own wife, the beautiful Irene Langhorne, of Virginia, as well as other society girls of the period whom he persuaded to sit for him. Mr. Gibson's girl had a great influence on dress and customs at the turn of the century. The puffed sleeves of her shirtwaist, her soft pompadour, her lovely feminine features were seen on everything from silver spoons to sofa cushions. She was the pin-up girl of 1900. Thus it is quite natural that the Royal Doulton Company, of Lambeth, England, should have used the Gibson Girl drawings for a series of plates made for the American market.

These plates were ten and half inches in size, made of porcelain and printed in black on a blue background. The first set, based on the series of pictures known as *The Widow and Her Friends,* consisted of twenty-four subjects, each with a caption, date, and Gibson's signature. The topics cover the period of his heroine's life when she was a widow and trying to reestablish herself in the world she knew. Following is a list of the subjects:

She contemplates the Cloister (*see* photo section).
She decides to die in spite of Dr. Bottles.
Exercise does not improve her spirits.
Miss Babbles, the authoress, calls and reads aloud.
She seeks consolation from her mirror.
A quiet dinner with Dr. Bottles.
A message from the outside world.
Some think that she has remained in retirement too long; others are surprised that she is about too soon.
Hostile criticism comes her way.
Mrs. Diggs is alarmed lest the widow ensnare her son.
She looks for relief among her books.
She longs for seclusion and prepares for a journey.
She is greeted at her journey's end by her six admirers.
She sketches under their gaze.
They all go fishing.
Failing to find rest and quiet in the country, she decides to return home.
Mr. Waddles arrives too late at the ball and finds her card filled.
She becomes a trained nurse.
She takes a morning horseback ride, her admirers following.

Miss Babble brings more criticism.
They all go skating.
She goes to a fancy dress ball.
She is disturbed by a vision of herself as a bride.
She renounces the world; her six admirers take Holy Orders.

Of course, your goal as a collector is to find the full set, which is a possibility, even though these plates are getting scarce. The original price for a Gibson Girl plate was fifty cents. Today they are selling for $12 to $18 each. In spite of the ridiculous titles of some of the plates, they are appealing, of good quality, and certainly, though a novelty, are as indicative of their time as any other type of china of the period.

There is a second set of twelve Gibson Girl plates in a nine-inch size, with a different black-and-white sketch of a Gibson Girl head on each. A darker blue border used a repetitious heart and bowknot motif.

I remember that my mother had one of each size on her plate rail. Another novelty plate on our rail was a *calendar plate*. These, supposed to have been of English origin, appeared in America about 1906, and cover a period up to 1929. They are, however, still being made in England, are marked Royal Staffordshire, and are sold over here in gift shops. These are being picked up by collectors to extend their sets of the older ones. Many of these plates were patriotic in character, with flags, globes, historic scenes. Others were merely "pretty" with the usual floral decorations of the 1900 period. Many of them were giveway or advertising items with the name of the store or product on them. They served the same purpose as the small Wedgwood tiles put out by earlier business firms. The calendar was either printed by months around the border or was concentrated in the center of each plate. The year, of course, is clearly indicated. They are not worth much from the viewpoint of quality or beauty, but they do not cost too much, $5 to $7.50, and they make an interesting hobby for those who like to pursue the elusive piece to make up a full set.

ABC plates have been made for a long time and in many materials other than china or pottery, but I can't remember ever having one. I learned my letters from a primer. I have seen them, however, in tin, glass, and pewter, some crude and primitive, and some of better quality. Many Staffordshire potters put them out with pictures in the center to appeal to children and with the alphabet letters running around the border. While a lot of these appeared in the 1800's, many were reproduced for later distribution and were still used for the edification of the children around the turn of the century. In a 1913 catalog, china alphabet plates were advertised for forty-four cents a dozen! The design showed a nursery-tale picture in the center, and around the border was the deaf-and-dumb alphabet, with pictures showing the position of the hands and fingers for each letter.

A very desirable collectible from the 1890's is the *portrait plate*. Often the head of a woman or child was printed or hand-painted as just a pretty face, not representing anyone in particular. However, other subjects were chosen for these portrait plates, often reproductions of famous paintings, such as Madame Le Brun; a famous Madonna; or Queen Louise of Austria. The one in our house was *The Angelus* by Millet. These undoubtedly were sent over from England, France, Germany, and Austria, along with other foreign imported china of the time. They will show the country of origin on their undersides if imported after 1891. They run from $6 to $10, occasionally going as high as $15.

Several niceties of dining were introduced in the 1890's and early 1900's for special courses of the formal dinner. One was the *fish set*. It consisted usually of six or twelve plates, a platter, and, sometimes, a sauce boat. This set was often made of fine imported porcelain such as Limoges, Minton, or Austrian. (*See* photo section for Austrian Karlsbad fish set.) An old Macy's ad pictures a fish set of Austrian china, numbering thirteen pieces, at $4.89. Today one of these sets will cost at least $30 in an antiques shop, maybe more, according to the number of pieces and the quality of decoration. They were usually hand-painted, each with a different fish, such as skate, salmon, rainbow trout, each depicted in its natural habitat. Bone dishes were often set beside each plate during the fish course. These little crescent-shaped dishes in all the late varieties of china, from ironstone to fine porcelain, are favorites in the shops today. Many women buy them just because they make excellent ash trays.

Of the same genre as the fish sets were the *game sets*, again of French Limoges, English Minton, or German porcelain. A recent sale in a New York gallery, offering turn-of-the-century antiques from a fine estate, numbered among other porcelains from England, France and Germany a set of Russian game plates from Korniloff Brothers, Moscow, an old firm established in 1825, thus adding another name to the roster of countries that supplied our fine china at the turn of the century. Each plate in these game sets shows a game bird such as pheasant, red grouse, bittern; some picture game animals such as deer and hare. They are greatly desired by collectors and with good reason, for they are a decorative addition to any room. Costs are rising. At one time not long ago a good French game plate would bring $8, but now it is getting hard to find them at anywhere near that price.

Charming sets of plates with fruit decor, were intended for luncheon or *tea plates* and they were usually smaller than the game sets. These have been diligently collected for some years. Many were made in the hand-painted era. They were usually sold in sets of four or six for small parties, occasionally for eight or twelve. Sometimes you can find a full set, but they can be picked up singly. They are just as lovely used today for luncheon, salad, or dessert as they were originally. Single plates run from $8 up, and if they are marked they usually bring much more.

Another china collectible from this era, when certain things were *de rigueur* at table, was the *oyster plate*. When oysters on the half shell were the opening course for many a well-ordered dinner, it was thought more correct to remove them from the shell and place them on special plates with shell-shaped pockets to hold them. Today, of course, we serve them shell and all on ice. Therefore, these plates are charming relics of a time long past. They go back into Victorian days—a patent on one plate shows the date as early as 1878—but they lasted over into the 1900's. Variety among them is great. They are to be found among the finest china and pottery wares put out in the late 1800's, including Minton, Delft, ironstone, luster, and majolica. They were even made in metal. Sometimes an extra pocket in the center was included for the sauce. They are a favorite collectible with restaurateurs. One of the largest and finest collections to be assembled fills the walls of a fine old seafood restaurant in Philadelphia, Kelly's, now run by Mr. Samuel Mink, who is proud of his hundreds of oyster plates of every variety—and justly so.

What the United States made and used in the way of native china and earthenware in the new antiques period hadn't, in the main, much claim to distinction, except for such developments as lotus ware and Rookwood pottery. The best things were imported, but these provide the collector with much to choose from, a great deal of which is sure to increase in value as time passes.

CHAPTER 6

DOLLS, TOYS, AND GAMES

ALTHOUGH there is tremendous interest these days in old toys and dolls, toys have always lived under hard treatment and their lives have been short. Consequently, there are not many old toys around, even though from the middle of the 1800's the toy industry in America began to boom and great quantities of all kinds were made. Importation of dolls and toys from abroad up until World War I, especially from Germany, kept our manufacturers hopping, and by 1911 moves were being made to promote the home-grown toy industry in this country. One scheme was to sell the idea of toys as all-year-round products. Another was to promote the toy fairs where buyers from retail businesses could inspect the new lines. A third step forward was the professional guidance in the selection of good toys that would fit the child and his age. All these things built up the industry in this country to the peak it holds today.

Dolls

Doll collectors are as numerous as the sands of the desert and as dedicated as the followers of any new cult. Doll collecting ranks with buttons, coins, and stamps as a top hobby. The advanced collector does not have to be told what doll to buy if she can find it at a price to fit her purse. She—or he, because many men are interested in dolls—has many helps: new books, magazine articles, museums, clubs, both local and national. For the beginner and uninitiated, however, it might be well to investigate the dolls of the early 1900's, because they are fairly available at realistic prices and are worth collecting. These will not be the old wooden dolls, the wax dolls, the Greiner, or other composition-headed dolls, the early German china heads, or Parian bisques, the French Jumeaus or Brus or fashion dolls. These are the older and choicer items of the doll world and it takes money to buy them, often more than $100. But there are many fine dolls that were imported from 1900 on, and many that originated in this country, to tempt the beginning collector. In fact many who have been collecting for some time are now adding these later dolls to the older ones that are the hearts of the best collections.

A query I put to the owner of one of the largest private doll museums in the country (custodian of over 5,000 dolls) about what advice she would give a young collector, brought this unhesitating answer: "German bisques of the 1900's. They are still comparatively cheap and a good investment. They will be worth a lot someday." So I promptly examined the "German bisques," which I soon found out meant dolls with bisque (unglazed porcelain) heads on various kinds of bodies that originated in the German toy centers. I was puzzled about how to recognize them until I found out that they were usually marked with the names or initials of the makers and that you can look them up in one of the several books on the subject. (*See* Bibliography.)

Dolls made after 1891, like all imports, will have the name of the country of origin—in this case Germany—imprinted with the mark on head or body. The *Germany* was often added hastily to dolls made before 1891 but imported after that date. Occasionally it was neglected or left off. Look for the mark on the back of the neck, under the hair, or on the front base of the shoulders.

One of the outstanding firms who made these later dolls was Simon and Halbig, known by their mark of S and H. These German makers put out millions of dolls during their fifty years of manufacturing up to 1920. Some were very fine, some mediocre, some not too good. The collector will soon learn to differentiate between the various qualities after inspecting and comparing a few. Late S and H dolls had bodies made of thin fabric or kid. It is said that the Germans bought up glove scraps for the purpose. Sometimes the bisque had a slightly shiny look, not characteristic of bisque. Like most German dolls after 1880, they had parted lips with the teeth showing. Ears were often pierced. The eyes were fine, of blown glass, with delicately threaded irises. They glowed with expression. German dolls' eyes were always particularly good and were often exported to be used by other makers. Wigs were glued on over the open top of the head, supposedly to save weight for shipping charges. A good Simon and Halbig doll can be had for $25 today, though some will bring more.

Other names of this period include Royal Kaestner, Armand Marseilles (marked A M on the back of the neck), Kamerer and Reinhart (with the initials K and R in the point of a star of David), and Heinrich Handwerck, who has not been determined as either a manufacturer or designer or both. There are many, many more still to be found and identified. The better bisques have closing eyes. There is a "flirting eye" doll with eyes that move from side to side. All of these dolls are the kind that little girls used to find under their Christmas trees fifty years ago. If the dolls still wear the original clothes you can often date them that way.

Some late French jointed bisque dolls were sent to America in these years. A familiar mark was SBJ, standing for the Societé Bébé et Jouets, which was a combine of the earlier Bru and Jumeau French manufacturers. They also made the Eden Bébé about 1899.

A German firm named Kestner, in Thuringia, was responsible for some of the most popular dolls designed for the American market. They were imported from the 1890's on into this country by a New York firm, George Borgfeldt and Company. Among these German-American bisque dolls was the *Kewpie,* based on Rose O'Neill's illustrations in the women's magazines from 1909 to 1915 (*see* photo section). The first Kewpie doll was cast by Kestner in 1913. These delightful little cherubs with topknot, wings, and fat tummies, made a great hit at the time—and still do with the doll collectors. Most of the dolls were *au naturel,* but one series was made with enough of a costume to identify it with a character such as a cook, soldier, etc. There was also a little black Kewpie. One of the cutest is the Kewpie in the pose of Rodin's statue, "The Thinker." Later, many Kewpies were made in celluloid and over the years the wings were discontinued in the pattern. They can be found in many sizes and the average price is about $10 or $12.

Following in the wake of the Kewpies came another little comic figure of bisque, also made in Germany. It was called a *Happyfat,* a character created by Kate Jordan, as a feature for John Martin's book for children. The Happyfats appeared about 1915–1916. They were small, three and one-half or four and one-half inches high. Only the arms moved. A single lock of dark hair was painted on the head; it divided in the back into two locks. The billowing skirts or balloon-type trousers gave the figures enough balance to stand alone. Larger versions of the same doll were made by Louis Ambery and Son with soft bodies and composition hands and feet. Markings on the bisque dolls were blue paper labels. Not too many have survived but enough to set the collectors talking about them and looking for them.

Up to 1911, Germany dominated the doll market in this country. But when World War I cut off the imports from that country, American manufacturers began to supply the need. One of the most successful triumphs at the time was the *Schoenhut* doll. These dolls were made in Philadelphia by a German immigrant, Albert Schoenhut, a descendant of German toymakers. His original doll was of wood, turned on a lathe, the head and face finished by hand. Metal joints enabled the doll to assume any position. It was sixteen inches high, strong and durable, and could be stood upright by a metal stand that fit into the foot. It was one of the most practical dolls yet made in this country. The hair was carved or supplied with a wig. The faces were "character" faces, painted realistically. Later on, other sizes were made and a line of infant dolls was introduced, also a walking doll. The last line of Schoenhut dolls made before the company went into bankruptcy in the 1920's cheapened considerably; the steel joints were no longer used and the bodies were made of cloth. But today any Schoenhut doll is worth buying if you have to pay as much as $25 for it. The walking doll will bring $50 or more. (*See* photo section for examples of Schoenhut dolls.)

A doll that is receiving a lot of attention at the moment is the *By-Lo Baby*. This infant doll was also made by Kestner, in 1924. The creation of Grace Story Putnam, it was called the Million Dollar Baby because of its popularity and the great numbers made. The first ones, with a bisque turning head and a composition body, proved so expensive to make that later on Mrs. Putnam adjusted her design to making a bisque head with a flange or rim that could be sewn or attached by wire to the soft kid body. Other factories beside Kestner made it. It was also made with a composition head. The Grace Story Putnam dolls are all marked. By-Lo babies are bringing good prices today. They run from $10 to $50 or more for a dressed baby with a bisque head.

As early as 1892, Sol D. Hoffman came over from France and started an American doll business making what he called *Can't Break 'Em* dolls with extra hard composition heads that really could not be broken. They revolutionized the American doll industry. In 1909, E. I. Horsman, a toy manufacturer, soon to become one of the big names in the doll business, put out his *Billiken* doll with a *Can't Break 'Em* head. It was his biggest hit. Many of us can remember this little grotesque figure, used in many ways as a talisman, that was supposed to bring good luck. It was Horsman who got the sole rights to make the Billiken doll. The verse that went with it is interesting:

> If you would have me stay with you
> And like to have me play with you,
> Be very sure that you are good
> And always act just as you should.
> I love obedient girls and boys.
> I am KING of all the toys—
> BILLIKEN

Good advice and good advertising!

In 1911, Horsman brought out a Campbell Kid doll based on the little figures made famous by the soup advertisements. They were revived forty years later.

An American company, a giant of the toy business, was the Ideal Toy Corporation, established by a small toymaker who is credited with making the first *Teddy bear* in 1903. While not a doll, this cuddly toy really belongs in this discussion, for it is an important part of our American cuddle-toy history. It followed the incident that occurred in Mississippi in 1902, when President Theodore Roosevelt refused to shoot a small bear cub. The story was played up by the newspapers, and Morris Mitchum, owner of a small toy shop in Brooklyn, got the idea of making a small stuffed bear with movable arms and legs that he called Teddy's Bear. He did not stay the sole maker of these bears for long. Every other toymaker got into the act, including Horsman, Selchow and Righter, and S. D. Hoffman of the American Doll and Toy Company. The Teddy bear got to Germany very soon, where it was made by Frau Margarette Stieff, a toymaker of Wurttemberg, who claimed to be the first to see the possibilities of a plush toy based on the newspaper cartoon depicting Roosevelt's humane adventure. But in spite of the controversy, and the competition in America, Germany, France, and England as well, Morris Mitchum went on to develop, with the help of his son, B. F. Mitchum, the Ideal Toy Corporation, which has become the largest doll manufacturer in the world, thanks to its beginning success with the Teddy bear.

It is easy to note the change in the Teddy bear figure. The early ones had longer, thinner bodies but with prosperity they put on weight and became plumper and more cuddly and appealing.

Mitchum's son was the maker of the famous Shirley Temple

dolls in a line of *"name" dolls,* popular in the 1930's. Among them were Sonja Henie, Fanny Brice, Charlie McCarthy, Jane Withers, and the Dionne Quints. Doll collectors welcome them to add to collections of much older dolls. It is hard to pinpoint prices for many of these late dolls because they have not yet stabilized, and the collector is apt to pay what he is asked if he wants a doll badly enough.

An attempt to fill the gap after German bisques stopped coming into the country during World War I was made by the Fulper Pottery of Flemington, New Jersey, who, from 1918 to 1921, turned out some very fine heads in bisque, including babies, small girls, small boys, and young ladies. It is said that they made about one hundred heads a day, which would presume that there should be many of them left. Many doll manufacturers bought them. But today the authentic ones are scarce, and have become real collectors' items.

Many dolls were linked up to the advertisers, such as the Toni, the Johnson and Johnson, and Smokey Bear. They are recent additions to the list of novelty dolls, but any collector would be unwise not to buy them whenever he finds them. Someday they will be sought as avidly as the earlier dolls.

At the turn of the century many artists created doll patterns and sold them to the fabric mills to be printed upon cotton cloth from which they were cut out, sewn together, and stuffed at home. There were legions of these soft, cuddly *rag dolls,* which included animal figures as well as human. Palmer Cox, creator of the Brownies, patented twelve of his Brownie characters to be printed for these rag dolls (*see* photo sections). Many were advertising items given away as premiums, which does not detract from their value today. Aunt Jemima, the trademark of the pancake mix, was given away as a premium for one box top and twenty-four cents in stamps. Dollie Dimple was printed on the sack in which flour was sold. There were Cream of Wheat dolls, Force's Sunny Jim, and a Ceresota Flour Boy.

Comic strip characters, such as Foxy Grandpa, and Buster Brown with his dog, Tige, were sold by the artists to the fabric printing companies to be made into dolls. Some rag dolls were printed on sateen with more colorful and elaborate markings. There was a jointed rag doll about 1900. The story-book characters of the time, the Golliwog, and the Raggedy Ann-and-Andy pair, came to life in do-it-yourself rag dolls. Sometimes a stuffed rag doll shows up at a sale or on the counter of an antiques shop, but the mortality in them is high. Occasionally, you can even find old lengths of yard goods printed with these patterns and never cut into. They are also being copied and reprinted today, and while of no antique value are fun to buy and make.

But perhaps the best rag dolls of all in America were those made by Martha Chase of Pawtucket, Rhode Island. Mrs. Chase had been so impressed in her own childhood by the famous Izannah Walker rag dolls, with faces painted and modeled in relief, classics in the doll category, that she started making dolls for her own children about 1891. They were so successful that the Chase Stockinette Doll eventually became a national industry, which is still carried on by the Chase family today. Mrs. Chase never got a patent for her dolls but they are all carefully marked with a label that reads, "The Chase Stockinette Doll, Made of Stockinette and Cloth. Stuffed with cotton. Made by hand. Painted by hand. Made by especially trained workers." The faces of the Chase dolls look more like real children than the usual empty doll faces do. After World War II, these dolls were made for use as hospital training models for the Red Cross, for health departments, and for home economic classes. New fathers being taught how to diaper and take care of the baby today often learn on Chase dolls.

Toys

The tale of toys in the first years of the 20th century involves an almost continual skirmish between foreign manufacturers, particularly those in Germany, and ourselves. For the brief period of World War I, however, when imports stopped, American firms tried to establish themselves more securely in the toymaking business. After the war the Germans attempted a comeback, and the situation was extremely competitive for some time. But American financial knowledge and ingenuity finally won out, and some firm names that rose to top the list then still remain prominent.

Toy collecting has long been a favorite hobby with men, and while the enthusiast usually goes in for the old and primitive (when he can find them), he is far more apt to collect the toys made in the late 1800's and after 1900, because they are more indestructible and were mass-produced in greater quantity. Consequently, they are more available—but they are not cheap.

The vogue for *iron toys* in which many collectors specialize began some years before the turn of the century, but it went on after 1900, with new toys reflecting the new inventions, such as trolley cars, automobiles, dump trucks, newer-type fire engines, buses, and the popular circus wagons. Any iron pull-toy today is almost worth its weight in gold. Let me insert an observation here: perhaps I imagine it, but it seems to me that any class of antiques that interests men always brings unusually high prices, the implication seeming to be that, to the

male collector, money is no object when he finds something
he wants. A woman will characteristically give it thought and
shop around and perhaps try to do some bargaining, thinking
all the time of other ways in which she might use the cash.
She shops for antiques the way she markets, often on a budget.
A man's hand goes to his pocket or his checkbook without hesitation when he sees what he has been looking for. To men,
antiques are often investments much like blue-chip stocks, and
men seem to like to boast about what they have paid for their
acquisitions, rather than boasting of their bargains as women
do. Needless to say, the antiques shops thrive on this kind of
business.

As examples of high prices, few iron pull-toys in good condition can be found under $50. There were a few wind-up tin
toys in this period, such as the "leapin' Lena" auto (1920),
trolley cars, buses, and so on, that come cheaper but are not
as available.

But of all the toys of the period, nothing is more favored
by the male collector than *electric trains*. These are true 20th-
century items. The first toy trains that ran by electricity were
powered by batteries, the earliest about 1896. But until house
current of the AC (alternating) type came into use, trans-
formers could not be used to adapt the home current to run
small trains. One of the earliest to add an electric motor to
his trains was E. R. Ives of Bridgeport, Connecticut. Ives advertised that the firm was the first to manufacture model trains
that would run on tracks. Ives trains are highly prized by collectors today. An Ives Electric train was recently advertised
for $44.

In 1906, Joshua Lionel Cowan, who gave his middle name
to his electric trains, added a transformer to his engines to
reduce the current to low voltage. Ives used O gauge for his

tracks, which was one and one-quarter inches in width, but Lionel trains at first were made to fit Standard gauge, two and one-eighth inches in width. Later on, most manufacturers of electric trains used the smaller HO gauge that made it possible to set up a more elaborate railroad in smaller space. As the years went on, Lionel added more and more features—box cars, coal cars, gondolas, Pullmans, oil tanks and other things, as well as bridges and tunnels. Setting up the family train before Christmas on its big platform, with houses, greenery, signal lights, bells, is as much fun and as significant for this modern age as was the old-fashioned *putz* or village years ago. It was not fun for me one memorable Christmas, shortly after my husband had died. He had started a train set the year before for my two small boys, and on Christmas Eve I got it out and looked at it helplessly. It would have been a defeat except that most unexpectedly a young divinity student, home for the holidays, rang my bell and, out of the goodness of his heart and filled with the Christmas spirit, offered to help me. It did not matter that he did not know a screw driver from a chisel, but his presence was enough to help me unravel the intricacies of the small Lionel set.

An electric train called the American Flyer made in Chicago gave the others a run for their money. In 1930, Lionel and the American Flyer bought out the Ives Company, and later, Lionel operated the combine. When the American Flyer fell out of favor during the depression, it was bought by the Gilbert firm of New Haven, Connecticut.

A. C. Gilbert was one of the giants in the toy business. While working for a medical degree in college, he started to make magic equipment. He soon gave up the idea of medicine to devote himself to making toys. His Erector set, put out about 1913, proved a best seller, challenged only by Mechano, an

English product. Gilbert finally bought out the American plant of Mechano. At a time when people were beginning to think of toys as aids to education, Gilbert brought out a series of educational toys in 1920. The first was a chemistry set, to be followed by microscope sets, weather sets, pneumatic engineering sets, and others. All Gilbert toys were well made and outstanding in the field. I happen to have known personally a most ingenious Philadelphia inventor who worked for Gilbert. Like most creative men he was temperamental, so much so that Gilbert transported him and his whole family to a fine home on the grounds of the company plant in New Haven, where Gilbert could keep this genius under his thumb and working.

Another top name in the toy market was Louis Marx, who established his firm in 1921. With the exception of dolls and wheeled goods, Marx made everything in the toy line and was without doubt the largest toy manufacturer in the world, with six factories in the United States and more in other countries. The electric trains he put out were cheaper than Lionel's. His outlets were the five-and-ten-cent stores and the mail-order houses. His was truly a mass-production concern. Old Marx-made toys bring good prices today, running up into the $20–$30 class.

Early in the century, about 1903, one of the most original and popular toys was put out by Schoenhut, the firm that later made the dolls of that name. It was the *Humpty-Dumpty Circus.* (*See* photo section for two Schoenhut circus figures.) The figures were of painted wood, articulated and strung with rubber. They could assume all kinds of poses. Slits in the wooden feet made it possible to balance them on ladders and chair rungs. A Humpty Dumpty in the largest and most complete set could include twenty or more pieces. There were the ringmaster, acrobats, lady horseback rider, clowns, elephant, donkey, lion, zebra, hippo, tiger, buffalo, giraffe, sheep, ladders, chairs, and stands. Extra figures could be bought as needed. It is seldom that a whole circus can be found intact today, but the little figures can be picked up separately, and they bring a pretty price. With the paint in good condition and the simple cotton costumes intact, they sell for $9 to $10 a piece. It would cost several hundred dollars to assemble a whole circus today if one could find all the figures—a big rise from the original price of $1 to $4 a set.

These were the years of the beginning of many trademarked toys, many of which still sell in the toy departments today: Lincoln Logs; Diabolo (1907); the Yo-yo; Kiddie Car (1920); and Tinker Toys (1914). Cap pistols and other exploding toys (*see* photo section for examples) were favorites with young boys during the turn of the century, and with some collectors today. Magic lanterns were at their peak from 1890 to 1910, but they were giving way to projectors that enlarged pictures on the screens, and to animated pictures run through a machine such as the Kittiscope, put out by Selchow and Righter, in 1908. Many were German imports. Prices for these lanterns run from $18 to $30 according to size and condition. The glass slides are also collected, many amusing, some artistic, but all of interest to the collectors.

Mechanical banks were in demand long before the turn of the century, but children were still being urged to save their pennies in these amusing toys until well into the 1900's. The J. and E. Stevens Company, of Cromwell, Connecticut, was one of the largest producers of these penny-savers, and are said to have put out fifty subjects from 1870 to the beginning of World War I. Some of their later numbers reflect the events of the times, such as the Artillery Bank; the U.S. Navy Bank,

of the Spanish-American War years; Teddy and the Bear, about
1902; and the North Pole Bank, put out in 1909, commemo-
rating Peary's discovery. Age does not dictate the prices of
mechanical banks so much as rarity. While the North Pole
bank brings around $800, and the Teddy and Bear bank brings
only $75, and is ten years older, the latter is not so scarce as
the North Pole bank, thus the difference in price. The tragedy
is that all these banks are being heavily reproduced, and very
skillfully disguised even to the worn-off paint and rust, so that
a collector must have his wits about him when he buys. This
is another male hobby that features prices running up into
the thousands. The top is still, I believe, the Columbine and
Harlequin, which was last quoted at $3,250. The lowest will
cost at least $35; Always Did 'Spise Dat Mule, one of the com-
monest, brings about $50.

Still banks, the ones that did not move or do anything but
retain the money, also reflected the times, and many are being
collected that date after 1900. Collectors staggered by the prices
of the mechanical banks are turning to the still banks as more
readily available and cheaper. One can find many topical symbols that were made into banks, such as the Billiken bank
(*see* Dolls); General Pershing; Radio; G.E. Refrigerator; and
World War I soldier, which brings them into the 20th-century
picture. Prices here run $5 to $15 according to subject.

Games

Before radio and TV, indoor games were top home amusement and most homes had a closet full of them for both young
and old. Bridge was not generally played before 1900, even in
its earlier version, which was called whist. Playing cards were
still frowned upon in many circles as "instruments of the

devil." Evangelists preached against them. This gave an impetus to the innocuous board-games and picture-card games. The vogue for such home entertainment began in the 1800's, and many toymakers added games to their inventories. One of the earliest game-makers was John McLoughlin, a lithographer, whose firm was established in 1808. His business was eventually carried on by his son and grandsons and finally was bought out by Milton Bradley, known primarily for kindergarten material, as well as for games, both before and after the turn of the century. McLoughlin, one of the first to make paper dolls and paper Valentines, also made many well-known games such as jackstraws, and cheap editions of older games.

Ives, known for his electric trains, also made games in Salem, Massachusetts. Authors, one of the oldest American games, was an Ives publication. A successor to Ives was Parker Brothers, established in 1888. This firm is still a top producer of games and many that are still on the market were first made before 1900. By 1898, Parker is said to have issued three hundred titles in the game field. Camelot, a relatively new game, has its ancestry in an old game of Parker's called Chivalry, which came out about 1917. Rook appeared just after the turn of the century. Pit and Flinch were Parker games. All these games are sought by collectors if complete, and show the date of issue. Someday, perhaps, even Scrabble (made by Selchow and Righter) and Monopoly (a Parker creation) will be added to the collections.

A major item that collectors are looking for are the old *Mah-jongg* sets, the Chinese tile game that gave bridge merry competition in the 1920's. Fortunately, these tiles, handsomely made and boxed, still linger on, thanks to their durability, even though mah-jongg is no longer a popular pastime. A good mah-jongg set can cost $15 to $20.

Marbles is a very old game and little boys around the turn of the century enjoyed their leather bags full of marbles just as their fathers had. But today marbles are not so popular as they deserve to be. There are too many other things for little boys to do, what with TV, Little League games, soap-box derbies, Scouts, and other activities. Little boys still play them in Mexico, and the craftsmen there make use of them in their lovely tin pieces. But here it may be the twilight of marbles, as it is for the jacks (jackstones) that little girls used to play with. I can remember playing jacks on the white marble steps of our Philadelphia home. It was exciting to see how far you could go without a miss as you grabbed a handful between the bounces of a rubber ball. The grabs were called one-ums, two-ums, up to ten-ums or even more. They sell now in the shops, but not so readily or for so much as marbles.

Fine marbles, the carnelians, swirls, and sulphides bring good prices, sulphides particularly (*see* Chapter 4, paper-weights). Most swirl marbles were imported from Germany where they were made from about 1876 to 1926. American factories did not make this type, but there were several firms in Ohio mass-producing cheaper "rainbows" and "shimmies" at the turn of the century. "Cat's eyes," a cheap marble, was made from bits of used glass. The first machine for making marbles in this country was invented in 1915. Although the little common, opaque clay marbles are worth very little and sell by the boxful if at all, all marbles are worth collecting, from those made of the finest semi-precious stones such as carnelian, jade, onyx, jasper, and cobalt, to the "steelies" of brass or iron. This is a fine hobby for men and boys, and takes little room to store or display.

How long it will take space-age toys to become antiques can-not be determined, and most of them are so poorly made that they probably won't last in quantity, anyway. In the meantime, there are plenty of good toys dating back to the new-antiques period that are unique enough to warrant their being collected, and of an age and quality to be on their way to becoming genuine antiques of tomorrow.

CHAPTER 7

THE GOOD OLD DAYS

MANY old things are being bought today out of a deep feeling of nostalgia, a desire to create the atmosphere of what we sometimes mistakenly call "the good old days," before automation, coexistence, delinquency, and cold wars brought new fears and a general feeling of uneasiness all around us. A rosy glow surrounds the picture of life as it was fifty to seventy years ago: leisurely; comfortable, if not always luxurious; and peopled with individuals of integrity and honesty. Right now this nostalgia is apparent in some of the reproductions that are appearing on the market, especially in furnishings. It is a wistful swing back to things associated with an easier life.

We see reproductions of brass beds, bamboo and wicker furniture, bentwood rockers, dome lights, and other reminders of the past being sold in the furniture departments of the shops and mixed in skillfully with the latest developments in the modern trend. But if you prefer antiques, go out and look for the real things, rather than the reproductions, that bring back the memories and tastes of fifty years ago. The things you buy may not be beautiful, nor truly valuable, and sometimes may not even be useful in their original way, but they can be entertaining, and can relieve the cold, unlived-in look of our modern homes. And most of them are interesting and fun to collect.

As antiques the worth of all these nostaglic items is more or less negligible. You won't find much quality here to carry them along the years, or chance of increase in worth, or possibilities of profit for resale. They are not the kinds of things, generally, that you will buy to sell later on. The prices asked today are no indication of true worth. In fact, the market for many of the things I will mention in this chapter has not stabilized as it has in other classes of old things, such as china and glass. Prices vary from shop to shop, or individual to individual. For that reason I cannot give you prices in every instance. It usually boils down to what the individual dealer or seller wants for a piece or thinks he can get. You can't even go by the bids you hear at the public sales these days because the competition often forces the price of a piece way up beyond what you would have to pay in an antiques shop just down the street. There is no yardstick to go by, only the popularity of the moment. As I've said before, there are no bargains today in antiques, only in the things nobody wants—yet!

These old things I am going to discuss and suggest for a few pages are not the kind to be found in the city galleries and auction rooms, or most city antiques shops, but they are the stock-in-trade of small-town and country shops. You'll find them at country auctions and those regular weekly sales that are half antique and half junk. You will find some dealers at

the antiques shows, even big ones, who specialize in purely
nostalgic items, often calling them primitives. Sometimes you
can find what you want in the advertisements of newspapers
or in the pages of the antiques magazines. If you want nostalgic items from around the turn of the century you can find
them, but it may well be up to you to determine how much
you want to pay for them.

Kitchen Items

The kitchen is where many of these so-called "new antiques"
end up. If there is anything more modern than our kitchens
today, it would be hard to find it, unless it is the bathroom.
Both rooms are primarily functional, and industry tries hard
to help in this direction by providing all kinds of new materials, electrical equipment, stainless steel, and plastic surfaces
that can be kept absolutely clean and hygienic. But I sometimes wonder, when I see a picture of a new kitchen or examine one in a newly built house or in a modernized home, if
anyone really cooks in them, if the odors of old-fashioned
vegetable soup or freshly baked bread ever waft through them,
or if anything ever comes out of the wall ovens except a
warmed-up TV dinner. I am sure that today, in new houses
or apartments, many women feel the same way about this
room, which once was the core of family living. This may help
to explain the rush that is on to buy up odds and ends of old
kitchen things.

We seem to have come full circle from Victorian days when
it was a symbol of lack of status to eat in the kitchen, when
"nice" people always ate in the dining room. Now we have
done away with daily eating in a formal dining room to a
great extent, and often do most of our dining in the kitchen

or family room, or a nook that is part of the kitchen. But we take some decorating steps to make the kitchen pleasant as well as practical, and this is where turn-of-the-century kitchen accessories can help enormously.

Where did the old coal or wood stove go when it gave way around the turn of the century to gas for cooking purposes? It was probably put to pasture on the farm or in the summer cottage where there was no gas. Or it was bought up by the itinerant junkman for old iron. But what was used on the old coal stove is still around in the antiques shops for you to buy and perhaps use in the old way or in a new one. You'll find waffle irons that fit into the opening of a stove top, iron gem pans, popover pans, cornstick pans, and iron tea kettles. They look out of place hanging on the walls of an antiques shop, but perhaps you, like I, prefer iron, for certain purposes, to the aluminum and glass kitchen utensils that came along in the 1920's. I, for one, belong to the school that feels an iron Dutch oven is the only thing that can turn out a good pot roast.

People in 1900 still made their own bread, but with the swing to commercially baked bread in the next ten years, all the pans, including those cylindrical, corrugated ones, the bread mixers, mixing bowls, and bread boxes, found their way to the secondhand shops and from them to the antiques shops. To tell the truth, I am at a loss to know what people do with the old mixers—unless they actually use them for baking bread, which it is becoming fashionable to do again in the gourmet crowd. But I'm afraid they are given what I call the "cute" treatment, and are turned into planters or lamp bases. The same thing could be said for those metal canners that date back to about 1910, the kind with two or more copper-topped cylinders that fit over the filled jars to be set on a base filled with boiling water. If you're under fifty you probably won't recognize them when you meet them in the antiques shops. Sure, they can be made into lamps if you like way-out things.

But *preserve jars* are another story. They have history. They were first patented in 1858 by John H. Mason of Millville, New Jersey, who fitted a threaded-top jar with a metal screw top. The name of Mason and the date Nov. 30th appeared on jars for the next seventy-five years, although they were made by various companies who bought up the Mason rights. Ball Brothers, of Muncie, Indiana, formed a firm in 1880 to mass-produce these jars and have kept on making them ever since, with variations in shape and lids. The town of Batsto, New Jersey (once known as Crowleytown and now part of the state-owned Wharton tract), is considered the home of the Mason jar, as the first one bearing the impressed patent date was blown there in a small glass-house owned by Samuel Crowley. If you are thinking of joining the ranks of the Mason jar collectors—and there are many—look for dates, names of companies, variety of caps, and shapes—the square-shouldered jar was the earliest. Most you will find today are less than seventy-five years old. But perhaps this doesn't matter, perhaps you are one of those who simply like the deep aqua color of an old jar and want to use it for other purposes: for flowers, for a bank, or to line up on your kitchen shelves as a decorative container.

Before the advent of the electric iron, sets of sad *irons* with handles were made to be heated on the stove top and used in rotation. You see them all over, sometimes for as little as $1 apiece, and unfortunately often painted in garish designs and colors. They are much better cleaned up and used as is. Following them were the irons into which a wooden handle was clipped, but these have no antique value. The older ones can be used very nicely, however, as book ends, door stops, and paperweights.

Both kinds of irons used a stand on which the iron was set while cooling or not in use. These *stands,* made of cast iron in various lacy patterns, pointed like an iron, raised on three legs and usually having an iron handle, are popular collectibles. Many people call them trivets and class them with true trivets, which were footed stands of either cast iron or wrought iron (earlier) of various shapes, used for holding hot pans, kettles, and dishes. I think it is better to keep the two names apart, for the iron stands were usually later and not nearly so artistic in design as the original trivets. They were often given away by the companies that made the iron sets, and sometimes had the initials of a company interwoven in the pattern. Women look for the various letters on these iron stands, hoping perhaps to find the whole alphabet. I don't know whether that is possible or not, but I do know that if you have a simple name, you can probably spell it out with iron stands on your kitchen wall. Iron stands can be found easily and for reasonable prices running from $2.50 to $4 or $5, and occasionally more for very rare ones. You can sometimes find dates on them, usually of the 1890's, though many were made earlier.

Kitchen articles of *tin* go as far back as the 1700's and early 1800's, and among the primitive tin pieces that are accepted as real antiques are the old candle boxes, the foot warmers, candle molds, candlesticks, reflector ovens, spits, plate warmers, coffee roasters, as well as the painted tin and punched or pierced tin so prevalent among the Pennsylvania Dutch. But tin was still used in the kitchen after 1900, before plastic replaced it. There has been a tendency for about twenty years to decorate old tin pieces, and often the efforts of the artist turned out well, but that enthusiasm has died down somewhat.

I suppose people got tired of it because so much of it was badly done. But good, old tin cleaned up is attractive enough in itself without the addition of painted designs. If you like tin, there are plenty of opportunities to use it in the kitchen. Old graters can be used to shield wall lights, a colander will dim an overhead light. Tin buckets and wash-boilers (some are part copper, beautiful when burnished) hold logs for kindling or old newspapers. A turk's-head cake tin will hold fruit around the center cone, which can serve as a candle holder. Bread and cake boxes can still hold bread, but are more likely to hold mending or old cleaning rags. You can do interesting treatments on the walls with scoops, pie lifters, nutmeg graters, and measures. Even the lowly milk can will double as a lamp base or an umbrella stand beside the back door. There was a tin clothes washer, a suction cup on a long handle, that you could use to advantage as a planter if you invert it. Use your ingenuity to put all the funnels, pudding molds, and spice boxes to work. Some dealers are very good at this sort of thing and get pretty prices for their efforts.

Perhaps you have an old *coffee grinder* handed down from the days when coffee beans were still ground at home in the belief that coffee was better if ground fresh daily and not brought home from the store already ground in a paper bag. You have the makings of a lamp here or a planter with vines trailing from the small open drawer. Or you can fashion yourself a novel conversation piece by using the drawer for cigarettes, and the metal bowl on top, where the coffee beans were poured into the grinder, to hold matches. These coffee grinders usually finish up well with a little sanding, staining, and wax or varnish. If you are lucky enough to find one with a pewter top, you will end up with a really nice antique. Prices on coffee grinders have risen. You will pay $8 to $12 or even more for a good one today.

Spice boxes are a good buy, either the individual small, square, or round ones out of a tin set or the whole sets of six or more in a lidded tin box. There are so many things you can do with them; use them for odds and ends on a desk, for sewing supplies, for an assortment of screws and tacks in a kitchen drawer. These tin boxes were usually japanned (finished with a brownish varnish), so maybe you will feel like touching them up with paint and adding a small cut-out before giving them a coat of protective shellac. They make fine cigarette boxes when decorated. Single boxes will cost about $1, a set about $5.

If you decide to collect tin *cooky cutters* you will not be alone. One of the first things women ask for in antiques shops today is, "Have you any unusual cooky cutters?" Most collectors soon get beyond the commoner ones: the chickens, horses, dogs, rabbits, birds, hearts, stars, ladies, and perhaps Christmas trees. But there are many unusual ones because these cutters were made by local tinsmiths, whose creative fancy might dictate anything. One of the rarest is the eagle cutter, which sells for as much as $15. Most of the others will run from $2 to $3 apiece. Keep your eye out for a pig, a frog, a peacock, a fish, or a feather. The old ones are heavier; some have handles and some do not. They make a delightful little collection and, what is more, can be used as well as displayed on a kitchen wall.

Don't pass by an old *slaw cutter,* if you see or recognize one in the shops. These are the implements used to shred cabbage, to make coleslaw or sauerkraut; they are wooden slabs with cutting bars of sharp steel embedded across the middle, over which the head of cabbage slides. You'll find a lot of them in the Dutch regions of Pennsylvania. They can be turned into wall sconces. If you are lucky enough to spot one of the especially large ones that was used for making sauerkraut, you can have the cutting bar removed and add legs to the box that held the cabbage head, thus turning it into an interesting coffee table.

A type of kitchen ware that is truly 20th century is *agate*. This is the speckled enameled metal ware, usually a robin's-egg blue, but found less commonly in green, yellow, gray, and an onyx brown. All kinds of kitchen pieces were made in agate ware—cooking pots and pans, tea and coffee pots, tea kettles, basins, pitchers, even plates and mugs. Sometimes it was combined with a pewter bottom, lid and handle, which made it handsome enough to come into the dining room. If you have your eye on such a piece, you can find one occasionally, but it will cost perhaps as much as $15 to $20. Other agate pieces run from $5 to $10. It is being revived now with a vengeance, probably because of its gay colors, and because there is enough variety in it to interest collectors. Be careful! It is being very faithfully reproduced for barbecue sets, much of it being brought from the Orient; it is often hard to tell from the original.

Wood was the first material used in colonial kitchens, along with crude pottery pieces. And it has proved its worth to the housewife for several centuries. In the early 1900's wood still had a place in the kitchen in spite of the advent of new materials. There is a charm to old used wood whether it is a butter paddle or a hutch table. So cherish any old pieces you may have or spot in the shops, leaving them as is, or refinishing them like furniture by cleaning, waxing, or varnishing them to give them a new dignity. You may want to do what many decorators are now doing, and arrange small wooden pieces on a large bread board for use as a wall piece—pop art if you

want to call it that, but usually a very pleasant way of displaying old wood.

If you leave the primitive and rarer wooden items such as
sieves, firkins, trenchards, tankards, and the like to the dedicated collector, you can still find plenty of homey things with
some charm and not too much age to be expensive that can
readily be picked up for kitchen decoration. Whoever would
think that the old wooden *potato masher* had any value? You'll
pay $1 to $2 for one now, for they have uses other than mash-
ing potatoes. They are being used as bases for chandeliers—
arms of tin, with light sockets at the end, are attached to them
and they are then electrified. This can be a do-it-yourself
project for the man of the house with the minimum of electrical experience.

There are possibilities, also, in old *rolling pins,* which sell
at sales or in the shops for a dollar or two. Collectors look for
the unusual ones, those with double rollers attached to a frame-
like handle; those without handles, such as the French chefs
still use; corrugated or impressed rolling pins with designs for
rolling out cookies; those inlaid with contrasting woods, all
usually made of maple. A few were made of colored or Nailsea
striped glass. You can use them for display, put hooks on them
for holding keys, or hang them on the wall for towel racks.
And speaking of towel racks, those old ones that hung on
brackets behind the kitchen door are being bought to come
out into the open and see a new life of use.

Most of the wooden things for making butter were well past
their heyday when the new century rolled in. Except in country districts, butter was no longer made at home. It was dis-
pensed in the stores in pound packages or dug out of tubs—
cheaper that way. Unless you want to go back to the 80's and
90's in your search for kitchen equipment, you will not con-

centrate upon the butter molds, paddles, buckets, and churns. They are true Americana and will cost in proportion to their rarity.

But don't ever pass up a good old *bread board,* round, oblong, or handled. They have a thousand uses. For making small table tops they can't be beat; the wood is usually thick and the ends of the wide plank have been given the familiar "breadboard" treatment by putting a narrow piece across each end, against the grain, to keep the piece from warping. Some boards with mottoes carved in the border, such as "The Staff of Life" or "Spare not, Waste not," were used at the table. These make fine wall plaques. Artists look for such boards of seasoned old wood on which to put primitive paintings.

Another useful item not to be scorned is the old *ironing board.* These boards, usually of pine, are very thick and are fine sources of old wood to have around for anyone doing his own furniture mending or restoring. Used on a proper base, such as an iron stove stand or even an old sewing-machine base, a tapered ironing board makes a good free-form coffee table.

One thing the kitchen has always had is the large *chopping bowl,* although today it is more likely to be used for salad. Keep your eye out for the old ones, hand-carved from maple or burl (the knot of diseased wood that grew out of the trunk of a tree and gave unusually fine markings of stripes and whorls). Later bowls were turned on a lathe from chestnut, pine and maple. Old round bowls as large as twenty or more inches in diameter can be found in the shops and will cost as much as $10 in the rough and up to $20 refinished. You can often tell the old ones by the marks left in the bottom from the food chopper. Both the round bowls and the wooden troughs, or oblong bowls (sometimes with handholds carved out at the ends), were more often bowls for mixing bread or

setting it to rise. Most old bowls will show stains from use that
are better left alone than tampered with. It is rather sad to
see a veteran of the kitchen varnished to within an inch of its
life, or—heaven preserve us!—painted. Just give an old bowl
a minimum of sanding to smooth it and clean it up a bit, then
wax or oil it. If you want it dustproof or waterproof, use a
coat of dull varnish instead of the wax. Nothing makes a
lovelier centerpiece for fruit or vegetables in an informal
setting than a battle-scarred old bowl. Or use them for sewing,
knitting, or general catchalls. Here is where true value lies
because you are dealing with handwork and special skills.
They are not a fad.

The lidded *sugar buckets* go farther back than 1900 but
were still pantry items even after that date. They make fine
kitchen pieces when refinished to hold almost anything. They
run $5 or more apiece. One bucket that is not as old as you
might assume is the sap bucket made for hanging on the sugar
maples when they were tapped in the spring. They show a
long stave, carved for a handle and were not too large, probably about ten inches in diameter. These buckets were used
until very recently, perhaps still are in some places. (When
you drive through Vermont in late March or early April today
you will usually see the trees neatly hung with plastic bags or
plastic buckets.) If you can pick up an old wooden sap bucket
for a few dollars, buy it. Refinished they bring $10 or more.
They make beautiful scrap baskets, among other uses.

Even *scrub buckets,* made of wood before the galvanized
tin, and, later, plastic ones replaced them, can often be refinished to make acceptable pieces, especially those that have iron
reinforcing bands. They make excellent scrap baskets or hold
papers or wood for the fireplace. There is not much value here,
nor in the small wooden tubs that people often salvage and

finish up for use on a patio or terrace. But they are useful and not offensive, even though scarcely antique. I have even seen one turned upside down and given legs to make a coffee table. How cute can you get?

In the shops or at country sales you can pick up other wooden pieces both with and without quality that lend themselves to refinishing, and are decorative or useful, such as old bootjacks, knife boxes, spoons, ladles, forks, scoops, and even stocking-stretcher forms.

Another thing you could interest yourself in if you are a "new antiques" collector, is *baskets*. Basket-weaving is an old art and one that continues right up to the present if we are to judge by the number of basket shops that you see along the highways. The new ones are surprisingly good but not to be compared with old baskets with the mark of years of use upon them. Those that survive the years usually hold up remarkably well. Don't buy any that aren't in good condition.

The commonest variety is the *willow basket*. Many country craftsmen used to grow special groves of willow for basket-making, using one-year shoots of varieties such as American green willow, the purple Welsh willow, and Caspian willow. The willow whips were dried and cured, then soaked well before using. Another common variety of basket was the splint basket. Splints were very thin strips or ribbons cut from a slab of wood on a "shave horse" or *schnitzelbank,* as the Pennsylvania Dutch called this type of bench that the worker straddled while he cut the splits. The wood used was usually oak or ash and, later, hickory. The Dutch were renowned for their basketry. They also made many baskets from ropes of dried grass tied or wound with stout cord. You'll find these varieties and many more in the shops, depending on the region in which you are searching. You can even pick them up at country sales.

Never pass up an old *clothes basket* if it is in good condition. Small or large, they can be put to many uses, as wood baskets, for toys, garden tools, even as a clothes basket! So much nicer than plastic. As useful containers they are superb —attractive, functional and durable. Many are quite antique, too. To treat an old willow basket, give it a scrubbing with a detergent or an abrasive household cleanser to remove the dust and grime of years, then hose it thoroughly. Water won't hurt it. It sometimes helps to swell and tighten the wicker. When it is quite dry from the scrubbing, give it a coat of glossless varnish for protection.

Women don't carry *market baskets* any more. They go to market in their cars and bring home the groceries in a carton or a big bag. But sixty years ago marketing had to be done oftener because there was no way of keeping things for any length of time. Even though there was more home service than there is today from butchers, dairymen, fishmen, icemen, and produce men, many women relied on the capacious market basket in which they brought home their purchases, which they had selected carefully with their own fingers as the frugal French women still do. The weekly markets still operating in many towns serve the same kind of housewife today, and the large, double-lidded market basket still survives. But many have been discarded and they are good buys when you find them. They make fine work baskets, magazine holders, and picnic baskets. Small lunch baskets and Easter baskets are also good buys, the latter usually of the grass variety in bowl shape or woven fancifully of colored straw. For fruit and flower centerpieces they can be used to create a dramatic effect. You'll find quite a few for under $2.

Mortars and pestles have a long history, going back to the days when all grinding, pounding, and powdering was done by hand. The colonists often brought their family mortars and pestles to this country with them, especially if they were made of bronze, as many were. They were considered precious enough to be passed on from generation to generation. In America they were made of stone, iron, brass, and wood, especially wood, usually maple or pine. Every kitchen, even today, needs a mortar and pestle, and if you can find a fine old one of turned maple or even one made at the turn of the century, so much the better. You can get them for $8 to $10, but a fine refinished maple might go as high as $15. They look very smart on a kitchen shelf.

When you go browsing in the antiques shops, keep your eyes open for old kitchen *pottery*. Everyone else is doing it, too, and you may have to do some looking for the popular pieces. Jelly or pudding molds of yellow-ware or white-ware, with various patterns in the bottom, are being collected by some women, and they make a fine showing along a kitchen shelf or hung on a kitchen wall. Did you know that even Wedgwood made white-ware molds? A yellow pottery rabbit mold was always used in my family for the Thanksgiving and Christmas cranberry jelly, and at no other time. It holds a place of honor in my own kitchen today. Of course, as you may have suspected, some women buy them for planters or flower arrangements. Prices run up to $8 to $10 for these.

Rockingham pottery, that brown mottled earthenware made in hundreds of factories across the country before and after 1900, sells for good prices in the shops and the better pieces are getting scarce. Many people call it Bennington, whether marked or not, because so much of this brown-glazed pottery was made at Bennington, Vermont, in the mid-1800's. But all kinds of similar earthenware was used for kitchen pieces long after this and well past the century mark. In color it varies from deep cream or tan to dark brown. There are many collectors of it. They have some interesting names for various varieties, such as "molasses" for the rich dark brown and "tobacco spit" for a lighter brown, which is mottled with patches of darker brown—not an elegant term but very descriptive. You'll find all kinds of pieces in Rockingham if you like it as well as I do: mostly bowls, small, large, and flat (for skimming cream); pitchers; mugs; teapots; coffeepots; plates. The collectors of this ware go all out for the earlier pieces for which they pay fancy prices. But the later kitchen ware that is being gathered up now is fairly reasonable, though prices are rising. A mixing bowl, ten inches in diameter, may run as high as $10, a turk's-head cake pan (the round fluted kind with a tube in the center like an angel-cake tin) about the same.

There is another type of kitchen pottery, not too old, that is called *spongeware* or sponged ware, not to be confused with spatterware, which is a much earlier importation about the time of Gaudy Dutch. Spongeware is pottery, mottled usually in blue on a grayish white ground, although you will meet it in other color combinations, with lighter blue grounds or tan or yellow-ware grounds with varicolored mottling. It was called spongeware because the dappling was actually done by dipping a sponge in the colored pigment and dabbing it on the piece. Like the Rockingham, this was made in all sorts of kitchen pieces, even tableware, and pitcher-and-bowl toilet sets. It was considered a common type of earthenware in its time, which was approximately in the later 1880's. It is durable, colorful, and naive, and lends itself to kitchen decor in a restrained way. Picture a large blue and white spongeware bowl filled with shiny red apples on a window sill. That bowl will probably have cost about $12. Of antique value or not, it is getting hard to find.

Stoneware, like Rockingham, was one of the earliest outputs of the American potteries. It was an old product in Europe, especially in Germany and England where the art of giving a sturdy hard-paste ware a dull glaze was accomplished by throwing salt into the kiln during the firing process. In America the same process was used for making all kinds of crocks, jugs, and pitchers to do heavy duty in kitchen or dairy. These are the pieces you can still see hanging around the outside of the roadside antiques shops to be sold for as little as $1 apiece. The better ones, of course, bring higher prices, particularly if they are decorated in some way or have the name of the pottery painted on them in blue. The colors are usually gray, tan, cream, and brown. The housewife had many uses for them —and so will you. The crocks were fine for homemade pickles, for cookies, or for putting down eggs in water glass (a preservative made from dissolving sodium silicate in water). The jugs were used for cider and vinegar. A big five-gallon crock was just the thing in which to make root beer for the summer afternoons. Today you'll use stoneware crocks for other things, to turn into lamps, for umbrella stands, and for plants and flowers. Zinnias in a fat brown crock are pretty enough to paint—and many artists have. Crocks with lids can be used in the kitchen as they were originally for things like flour, salt, sugar, tea, and cereal. They have a good primitive quality even when they were made in the 20th century.

Country Store Items

There has been great interest in the last few years in all the things sold in the country store of hallowed memory. As nostalgic antiques they have no equal. Not many homes in the populated areas around 1900 had to rely upon the general neighborhood store, but in the country the "emporium" still existed. One of the last to go on our city street was a store run by two very old ladies who had grown old with the business. I can still remember the smell of it, a mixture of many things dominated by the odor of the glossy finish of the cotton lining fabrics. Today, Irish whisky reminds me of it. But one thing I will never forget was the front counter, which Miss Libby told me had been part of a dining table that had belonged to her father when he was a sea captain. To prove it, she removed the candy jars, the penny dolls, the jumping jacks, the black cotton stockings, and a pile of rickrack braid and cards of shoe buttons and swept off the dust cover to reveal two halves of the most gorgeous Santo Domingo mahogany banquet table with carved legs. The old ladies died soon after, the store was closed, and I have wondered ever since what became of that table.

The great Atlantic and Pacific Tea Company, established in 1870, was beginning by the turn of the century to give the neighborhood grocery store a run for its money. The burgeoning Woolworth business (approximately 10,000 stores by 1911) was taking over the sale of the small items and novelties. Clothes, hardware, and furniture were bought in the department stores. In the country, the store at the crossroads was losing business to the mail-order houses. By 1930, the country store had practically disappeared, the last stragglers suffering themselves to be turned into self-service stores. A few lingered on, and, when they sold out, it was usually by public sale, where the prices were in line with all the auctions of thirty years ago.

As late as twenty years ago there was a country store still doing business in the village where I now live. It contained the usual things associated with country stores: a cracker barrel, checkerboard, wall telephone, and a pot-bellied stove, around which the ancients of the township gathered to discuss crops, politics, and juicy gossip. My young sons were fascinated with it, and, until I realized what was going on, they learned more than their prayers in the hours they spent there.

The country store could easily be nothing but a memory if a number of small museums across the country were not keeping the memory alive by recreating the authentic store scene. When you travel by auto you meet them wherever you go. Some charge a small admission, some sell part or all of their stock, some are antiques shops specializing in country-store items. Very often there is someone about to explain the bee veils, the buggy whips, the sun bonnets, and the slicers for cutting the chewing tobacco. You'll meet certain dealers at the antiques shows who deal in country-store items exclusively and are largely responsible for stocking these museums. These nostalgic items are not generally of much intrinsic value, but they are interesting as curiosities, and they cannot be ignored when discussing the things made and sold up to seventy-five years ago. A lot of information about the progress of this country can be traced through them.

It used to be that you could pick up bargains when an old store sold out, sometimes stocks of things still in their boxes and never used, as well as the fixtures. I have a pair of unused brass bracket lamps that I bought from an old store. I had them made into electrified wall sconces and the price was nothing like what I would have had to pay for new sconces. For years I have been picking up the little pottery pie plates, quite a staple in the country stores, for use under my pots of African violets. Once they cost fifty cents apiece, or less; now they sell in the antiques shops for $4 to $6. Other country-store items in my house are a bright tin comb case and mirror that hangs on the wall above a pair of old tin candlesticks, and a slant-lid coffee tin with the name of the maker on it. Its bright red coloring enlivens my hearth and holds my kindling. It cost $10 ten years ago. I was always going to paint it, but now I am glad I did not. It is much more honest and nostalgic as it is.

A large and desirable category of collectible are these *tin bins* and canisters used in country stores for holding coffee, tea, and other dry groceries, such as peas, beans, etc. If you come upon one with traces of the original decoration, which was usually a transfer print or lithograph, don't cover it up. Just paint around the worst part and touch up the rest. Some of these pictures, especially on the tea boxes, were Oriental in character and very attractive. You will find many of these old bins and boxes battered from use. But don't give up. They can be mended by a tinsmith if otherwise worth it. Sizes and forms of canisters vary. Some have a mirror at the front. Some have lift-up lids, some screw-on lids at the top. The bottom usually lifts up to get at the contents in the case of spice boxes. I have one with a roller at the top that revolves to bring into view a succession of names like allspice, ginger, cloves, cinnamon, making it useful for any one of these spices. These canisters are lovely to have in the kitchen today for holding supplies, such as cookies, soup beans, special flour, and so on. But mostly they are converted into lamps. They make very handsome ones, no matter what size canister you use. The very largest bins are often used as end tables. You can't buy a good canister under $5. Large bins, undecorated, run about $15 or more.

In a family with the bins and canisters are the old tin boxes that held commercial products—tea, crackers, tobacco, gunpowder, and various other things.

Tole was the name used originally for the painted tinplate of high quality that went into artistic household items. It was made in Pontypool, England, in the 1700's, and in France in the Empire period (1802–1825). Pieces made of this fine old material command high prices. The word tole continued to be used for all kinds of painted tin, no matter what quality, up until the mid-1800's.

What we call "new tole" is later still, and is not painted but decorated with transfer printing. All the pieces, including the canisters and commercial boxes, are desirable, but new tole embraces many other things, too: trays, plates, pitchers, some that were even used for advertising purposes. Transfer printing, as the china decorators found out, was a much simpler and cheaper way of decoration than handwork. Much tin was decorated in this way, and some of the results even on common pieces was often as fine as hand-painting. Even today we find decorated tin in boxes used for commercial purposes, especially the foreign boxes for cookies and such. I have seen a pair of fine Park-Frean (English) biscuit boxes made into attractive lamps. For myself I would never give up a small double-lidded tea box of quarter-pound size covered with a Russian scene. It belonged to my mother and I played with it as a child. When I realized what it was in later years, it went into display on my shelves of curios.

Scales were an important part of the equipment of the country store. Most of the scales sold in the antiques shops today come from this source, especially the iron ones with brass scoops; these stood on every counter for weighing out sugar, flour, dried peas, beans, before prepackaging took this job out of the hands of the storekeeper. Scales are far more valuable when the full sets of weights that went with them have also been saved. You can use an old scale most effectively as a table decoration when it is filled with fruit, or even with a mixture of colorful vegetables. Scales with brass scoops are far more valuable than those with tin scoops. You'll pay $20 or more for a good scale with a brass scoop. Often you can buy the scoops alone. If you are a scale collector you will not stop here. You'll be interested in special scales for weighing butter, scales for eggs, and even the old steelyards, which is the name for the kind the ragman used to weigh our rags or papers. Variety rather than appearance or usefulness counts more with the scale collector.

The old country store had all kinds of *measures,* mostly of wood or tin. Old feed stores supplied wooden iron-bound buckets holding half-pecks, pecks, and bushels. These and similar buckets used in the general stores can be cleaned up and the wood refinished; these make fine scrap baskets or receptacles for kindling, which you can use in any room that is not too formal in furnishing. Old pewter and copper measures go back to the early 1800's or before, but you can console yourself with a row of the less expensive later ones of tin used in the country stores, if you are collecting semi-antiques on a budget.

Scoops, tin, wood, and brass, are tempting buys among the country-store items. (*See* photo section for brass scoops.) You can have a good time finishing them up for some original use, such as serving bread or rolls, crackers, or snacks. Be careful not to overdo your refinishing. You don't want them to look like new, or like a reproduction piece. In most areas you can locate small replating shops where you can take old brass and copper for a good cleaning and shine-up, generally all you will need. (Some department stores offer this service in cities.) The same goes for pewter. I belong to the school that does not like my pewter so dark that it is almost black, but neither do I like it shined up to within an inch of its life. Just tell the man who is going to work on it how you like it. After a professional polishing, it isn't difficult to keep it that way.

One thing from the country store that you will be sure to want when you see it is a *bag filler,* the handy wide-mouthed metal funnel that was inserted into the mouth of a paper bag to keep it wide open while it was being filled with staples such as sugar or salt or coffee. They are usually brass (sometimes tin) and come in various sizes. You'll find them in the antiques shops. People buy them for wall planters. They plug up the bottoms and use them for artificial flowers or greens, or if for real flowers they insert a small glass or jar for holding the water.

Iron *string holders,* which were suspended over the counter or kept on the counter top, attract buyers today (*see* photo section). The counter item is usually shaped like a beehive and is just as good as it ever was for holding string in your kitchen or garden room. You can make a small night light out of the hanging type by inserting a small electric bulb into it and having it wired. It will give lovely, lacy shadows in your hall or on your patio. If you knit, you might try using one for your ball of wool. This is another item that is not particularly valuable but it is useful and can be interesting. The going price for them is $4 to $7, according to size.

The *coffee mill* with wheels for turning the grinder is a familiar object in antiques shops and antiques shows. Decorators convert them into lamp bases. Like lots of other items that have been made into lamps, such as nautical pulleys and blocks, large wooden wagon hubs, and toy stoves, they are acceptable for certain rooms where informality is the style, but they have no value as antiques. The tendency to turn everything that cannot be used as a planter into a lamp is to be deplored. Such things are fads and short-lived. After a time you get tired of seeing them around.

Cuspidors were still in use in the early 1900's and every country store sold them and provided them for their tobacco-chewing or cigar-smoking clientele. After this unattractive habit went out of style, many of the old cuspidors were discarded and eventually landed in the antiques shops. Most of them were of pottery or brass. The pottery items were of Rockingham, often made by Bennington, in Vermont, and so marked. Old stoneware cuspidors, with cobalt blue decorations like the crocks described in this chapter, are often quite handsome if you can forget what they were used for. You can get a really fine effect by using both the brass and pottery cuspidors for trailing vines.

A new antique that appeals to men is the *tobacco cutter* that was kept on the counter for cutting blocks of plug tobacco into small squares for sale as the customers wished. These are long-handled knives, hinged on an iron frame or platform. They vary considerably in shape and form. They are strictly collectors' items for those who go in for novelties in the tobacco category. A popular one has the name *Imp Thumbing His Nose* imprinted on it. What anyone could do with them except to display and gloat over them I don't know. But they sell in the shops. They run in price from about $5 for the ordinary kind to as much as $20 or more for the rarer ones.

Old *wall telephones,* still in use in homes and stores around 1900, have been bought up and commercialized. Some of the novelty they had when they were first unearthed from the junk shops has disappeared, but they are still being bought to be made into various things, such as cabinets for radios, or turned into real working phones. They are the essence of real nostalgia. Foreign phones from Denmark and France are competing with them. I'd call all of these a flash in the pan; ten years from now they will probably be forgotten.

One thing that has become so popular that prices on it have zoomed far above the worth is the commercial *spool cabinet* that was made with two or more drawers to hold sewing cotton and silk. It was always a thrill to see a drawer opened, when a cloth sample was to be matched, and be faced by a rainbow of colors arranged in the order of the spectrum. These cabinets were made of lesser woods such as oak or ash, usually stained to look like walnut or mahogany. But they can be refinished to look like fine old furniture and used in almost any room of a house that is not too formal. They are useful for many things that can be stored in the shallow drawers—prints, maps, jewelry, knickknacks, stationery, buttons (for button collectors), photos. Some of these cabinets have as many as fourteen to twenty drawers and are quite elaborate, with good knobs or handles and often a mirrored door. They make fine filing cabinets or repositories for flat table linen or flat silver. Most of them date from the late 1880's, but some were made and used up to 1900 and after. They usually had the name of the thread company on them, such as ONT or Belding, which has to be removed if you wish to make a really attractive piece of furniture out of your cabinet. Smaller ones are often put on a base or legs for use as an end table, or on higher legs for a desk. Use your judgment about how much effort to spend— and also how much money—on a spool cabinet. If you can find one in good condition and of good wood, it might pay to have a cabinetmaker do your work. I have just recently acquired one that was beautifully done. It has a cherry top, walnut frame, and drawer fronts of curly maple. The handles on the four drawers are the original brass bail handles. Set on a base with four straight legs it has become a really nice piece of furniture for my living room. It has the air of a period piece. This is one of the new antiques that I feel is worth looking for and following up. You'll pay $16 to $20 for a small one with three drawers in the rough. Mine cost $75.

There are many old *advertising signs* that interest the collector or the individual who likes amusing pieces for his recreation room. They have some value as records of early advertising as well as calling up memories of days not too long gone. Perhaps you will fall for the little Pears Soap girl, with her bunch of violets, saying, "Good morning, have you used Pears Soap?" Or a Spotless Town scene, with a limerick advertising Sapolio; or the genial Quaker Oats gentleman; or the scurrying Dutch Cleanser woman. The old Ivory Soap pictures with the slogan, "It floats," introduced in 1891 and commissioned to well-known artists of the day, such as Palmer Cox (of Brownie fame), J. O. Leyendecker. Jessie Wilcox Smith, and Maud Humphrey (mother of Humphrey Bogart), were given away with ten soap wrappers until 1890, and have value if they can be found today. These are older items, but later signs such as those for Postum (1897), and Jello (1897), will update the list. There is no standard price for these. They are even being reproduced and framed as gift items.

Political *posters* during the elections of Harrison, McKinley, Theodore Roosevelt, and Taft hung in the country stores where debates ran fast and furious. These are very much collectible as antiques of the future, along with other political items, such as parade banners and paper lanterns.

The country store was the only source of bought candy in many communities. All the small candies such as chocolate pennies, nonpareils, Boston beans (candy-coated peanuts), were scooped out of glass jars with small handled glass cups that looked like miniature beer mugs, and sold at so much a cup. These cups are sold in all the shops today and are worth buying because many were made in pressed-pattern glass (*see* photo section). Some were of colored glass. The idea is to assemble a matched set of four or more and use them for serving liqueurs. They used to cost 50 cents apiece; now they sell for $1 or $1.50.

Old store-counter *candy jars* are always a good buy. Those with tin lids are usually earlier; glass lids came later. You can use them for many things. The large ones make fine terrariums. I have seen them used at Christmas time to hold a gay assortment of Christmas-tree balls for holiday decoration. Prices range from $5 to $10.

There is another little country-store item that pops up in the shops often and is worth considering. It is a flat-topped little stand, really a small compote, made of canary-colored glass for displaying teaberry gum. It makes a nice serving dish to use along with your other colored glass.

One of the most interesting pieces of equipment in the old country store was the post office. Usually it was nothing more than a counter with a partition or front of numbered cubbyholes. R.F.D. put a stop to many of the country-store post offices, but a few are left. I can even remember one near me not so long ago. It was a sub-post-office station in an old store that remained as it was despite the city that had grown up around it. These cubbyhole *mailbox fixtures,* if they can be found, are excellent for use as room dividers or they can be used quite nicely for displaying a collection of small antiques.

You'll see them occasionally in antiques shops or at antiques shows. They are usually found in "in-the-rough" wood, or showing traces of old paint. Prices vary considerably.

Music Makers

Two big inventions changed the course of music in the home at the turn of the century. Music was no longer a do-it-yourself affair, with Mother at the piano, Dad scraping a violin, or Sister getting music out of a cottage organ. By 1900 you could turn a crank or work pedals and fill the house with musical sound even if you didn't know a note of music. No longer did the family have to rely for entertainment on listening to Junior's last "piece" given to him by his music teacher, or to Sister's pyrotechnical rendition of "The Storm," or the "Maiden's Prayer," played with crossed hands. The mechanical *player piano* and Mr. Edison's phonograph had come in.

The piano that actually played itself gave the parlor organ and the huge grand piano with its bulbous legs stiff competition. The original concept of a player piano was French. One was exhibited in 1876 at the Centennial Exhibition in Philadelphia, but the idea did not take hold in this country until the late 1890's. It flourished for about thirty years, until 1925, when radio put it out of business. The music for this type of piano came from perforated rolls that guided the keys, and it was operated by pedals and bellows, before it became electrified. The rolls, many of which were classical numbers, were often originally recorded by famous artists and resulted in something that was not purely mechanical in tone. Of course the home repertoire was limited by the number of rolls in the cabinet.

Many companies made these player pianos. Perhaps the

Aeolian Company's Pianola was best known, but there was
one called Angelus, made by Wilcox and White, and the
Cecilian by the Farrand Organ Company. You might wonder
where they all went to, but whether relegated to the second-
hand shops, junk piles, or cellars, they have emerged today.
The player piano is back with a vengeance, not only for lend-
ing quaintness and canned music to certain places of entertainment, but as collectors' items. They are amusing and certainly nostalgic. You may want to put one in your family
room. But you won't find one easily. It might be a good idea
to advertise for one in your local paper. Every month the magazine *Hobbies* devotes several pages to old musical instruments, and if this is an area of collecting that you are interested
in, it would be a good idea to follow both their articles and
the ads.

Business is brisk in old piano rolls. If you go by the *Hobbies*
ads, the demand seems to be for names like Duo-Art, Welte,
Ampico. There are also new rolls being made for both the
old and new player pianos, testifying to their revived popularity. Prices for both pianos and rolls are something you will
have to dig out for yourself. They are not standardized as they
are in so many other antiques.

For those who did not have a piano at the beginning of the
century, there was still the *music box,* long a center of interest
in the Victorian parlor. Collecting music boxes today is a very
special hobby, requiring research and money. Here is one nostalgic item where real value lies. They were the work of clock-
makers in France and Switzerland, and, later, in America,
pieces of fine scientific workmanship. The best-known boxes
made in this country, and well into the 20th century, carry
the names of Borland or Regina (with metal discs). The latter
company is said to have made 100,000 music boxes between

1894 and 1919, when the interest finally died out as other music makers came along to replace them. But as antiques they have held their value over the years and will continue to do so. Advanced collectors look for many things—the number of tunes played by the rolls or disks, other added effects like drums, bells, etc.—and prices vary accordingly. A good Swiss box, with drums, cymbals, and bells, can cost as much as $250 according to its condition and number of cylinders. The simplest Regina box, of which there were plenty around about ten years ago, now brings at least $150. People love the sound of these old boxes and buy them for pleasure as well as antique value. There is something soothing and pleasing about the tinkling music and the old tunes they play, especially the Christmas carols. In fact, recently, phonograph records of old music-box carols have been made just to recreate this delicate music of bygone Christmases.

Just about 1900, the first Edison *phonographs* with wax cylinders (invented in 1880) came into general use. They brought music and voices into the home in a big way and eventually became far more important than the music boxes or player pianos. With just a little winding, the mechanics of making music could be forgotten while the notes of a female voice singing "A Bird in a Gilded Cage" filled your living room. It was *live* music. Or the drawling voice of Josh Billings (the character created by the humorist, Harry Wheeler Shaw) could keep the family in stitches with his monologues. Sousa's marches were so stirring you could picture the parades somewhere beyond the wooden box. The first phonograph horns were so large that they had to be supported by wire stands. They were often shaped and painted to resemble huge morning glories.

Interest in old phonographs has mushroomed in the last few

years. Men, particularly, are attracted by them, and many have become experts on their history and development. Of course, the idea is to find those that still play or can be made to play, but if you need help to get them in working order, there are mechanics who specialize in their repair. An old Edison phonograph in good shape brings about $30 to $50 in a continually rising market. Often, the wax cylinders come with the machine, but of course, being fragile, many have been broken, scratched, or worn down. Dealers advertise old records, however (*see Hobbies* magazine), and there are still a lot to be had. One of the most complete collections of wax cylinders is housed at Syracuse University. Here is an item that will not fall off in value.

Some collectors prefer to buy the old hand-cranked disk phonographs that still turn up at country auctions. There are also collectors for the old records, which have established more or less stable price lists (*see* Bibliography) according to age, rarity, and recording artist. This is a highly specialized avocation that classifies more as a hobby than it does as antiques collecting.

Early radios, except for the first "cat's whiskers" types, hardly come into this period of the first quarter of the century, but they, too, are being collected today.

There are buyers for many old *musical instruments,* including dulcimers and zithers, in which modern folk singers have helped to revive interest. You can find them in the antiques shops, priced at as little as $15. A fine dulcimer might cost $25. Old banjos, of the five-string type, also have value as antiques; today's hootenannies have helped to revive interest in them. This was probably the most popular string instrument of the 1890–1920 period, until the ukelele came along. Old banjos marked Vega, or Vegaphone, are the concern of professionals.

You should never throw away *sheet music.* Somebody wants it, especially popular songs from the 1900's through the 1920's. Often, a collector will buy a piece of sheet music simply for the cover photograph of the singer who made it popular. You will not make a fortune selling old music, nor will it cost you much to buy it if you want to collect the old tunes, but it can be an entertaining hobby. Most pieces of sheet music sell for ten to twenty cents a copy, depending on condition and rarity.

Jewelry and Toilet Accessories

The jewelry of Victorian years is a great favorite among women buyers. It was often handsome, always interesting, and is still wearable today. It costs relatively little compared to jewelry made of precious stones. Victorian lockets, garnitures, brooches, of amethyst, garnets, cameos, seed pearls, jet, and coral, set in gold, plain, or worked or engraved, tempt the lovers of true antiques.

The jewelry of the turn of the century, however, was not really outstanding. (Costume jewelry, with its showy use of glass and ersatz gold or silver, had not yet come in, and it is doubtful if any of it will become antique in the future.) Small and daintier jewelry pieces followed the Victorian, using small pearls, chip diamonds, and marcasite. Among the few items from the jewel boxes of the early 1900's worth looking into are the long *watch chain* that ladies used for their lorgnettes, and the watches they tucked into the belts of their shirtwaists. The slides that held the watch chain together in a double strand are especially desirable. They were small and frequently jeweled with pearls or opals, and now you use them for bangles for bracelets or assemble five or six on a double strand chain to make effective bracelets or short neck chains. Jewelers are finding many original ways to make use of them. A chain (gold-filled) with slide will run about $10.

The small ladies' *watch* has come back, to be used either as a watch, if in running condition, or as a locket. If the works are beyond repair, the watch can be used on a watch pin as a blouse or lapel ornament. The front and back covers of the cases that show fine engraving or enameling have been turned into very interesting pins or clips. Any jeweler can do it for you. $25 will buy a good watch of this period. They never lose value.

Beads were popular in this period and are the closest approximation of the costume jewelry that was to come later. Many things besides glass were made into bead necklaces: strings of coral, lapis lazuli, moonstones, amber, jet, carnelian, agate, and crystal. Dealers specializing in old jewelry always seem to have a good supply of beads, especially amber, either in the opaque or clear cut type and varying in depth of color. A nice amber string will cost at least $25. Many women who have studied jewelry-making as a hobby make a practice of buying up odd beads when they find them, for setting into gold or silver hand-wrought pieces. You'll find the old bead box a fascinating one to poke into on the antiques shop counter.

Among pieces used by the men in this era that are popular collectibles of the moment are *watch fobs* and chains. They were a necessity before the appearance of the wrist watch, about 1921. While not as elaborate or as heavy as the watches and chains displayed across their waistcoats by the gentlemen of the Victorian years, these later ones from 1890 to 1910 have much interest. In this *fin de siècle* period, good taste toned down men's jewelry. The watch chain still stretched across the vest from pocket to pocket, but it was usually unadorned. The watch fob grew smaller. More men were carrying their watches in their trousers pockets; and these had fobs of gold-mounted black ribbon on them so that they could easily be pulled from the pocket.

Men still hung some items on their watch chains, such as penknives, or combs, or pencils, or cigar cutters, usually of gold, and all these are being sold today wherever you find antique jewelry. Many of the chains and fobs were of "solid" 14-karat gold but many more were gold-plated or of a gold-filled metal. When you go to buy such a piece, steer away from the inferior gold-washed items that soon became shabby as the gold wore off—or that will become so in time. You can't shine these up; they are simply worn out.

Fobs are of particular interest if they show good seals or other pendants. Many were set with stones—carnelian, amethyst, sardonyx, topaz, bloodstone—often cut intaglio with classical subjects. You'll have to shop for these for bangle bracelets and you'll pay at least $15 for a good one. The watch chains with interesting links are being bought to hang the bangles on. Many women are wearing the whole fob as a pin or ornament. Some collectors, usually men, are buying fobs showing advertising or fraternal insignia. These can still be bought for as little as $2.50, but as interest spreads they are bound to rise in price.

Every woman knows that fine earrings can be made from old studs and cufflinks, which is another reason for going through the old jewelry box or tray in the shops or at the shows. They know, too, the value of old tie pins, which they take to jewelers to make into fine lapel pins. Good tie pins will cost at least $5 today.

Among a man's standard belongings at the turn of the century were pocket *match boxes,* of which fascinating collections have been made. Before the advent of the match folder or the cigarette lighter, these were a necessity. The earliest match boxes appeared about 1830, in England, when the first friction matches were invented, but they continued to be used for almost a hundred years. The most interesting ones were the early boxes, figural in shape, made to resemble animals, books, bottles, guns, nuts, violins, and dozens of whimsical things. The later ones were purely functional, usually of silver, sterling or plated, or of brass. They were large enough to take the kitchen match and often had a rough spot on the bottom on which the matches could be struck. There are plenty of these around but all are not necessarily unusual. One of the usual silver-plated type can be bought for $5, or even less.

A cigar-smoking gentleman at the turn of the century kept a supply of cigars in his pocket in a useful and sometimes unusually decorated case. These *cigar cases* were of silver, papier mâché, or leather. You can find them around in the shops, and in good enough condition to be used today by any man who smokes cigars. (Many men prefer an old one to a modern case.) A nicely decorated papier mâché case will cost about $5.

On the lady's bureau in the early 1900's were many items that have ended up in the antiques shops. One was the *buttonhook*. (Buttoned shoes were still worn at that time.) There is not much antique value in the hooks, but there are enough varieties to make collecting them an interesting hobby. A patent date of 1875 has been found on one, but there is usually little to define them as early or late. They were made with handles of silver, gold, wood, ivory, mother-of-pearl, brass, and other materials. Many were given away as advertising items with the purchase of a pair of shoes. Sometimes men borrowed them to button up their spats. Gloves still had buttons, for which there were smaller hooks, or they were buttoned with the aid of stiff loops of wire mounted on a short handle.

Several other items from the bureaus at the turn of the century have become part of this new antiques picture. One was the *hair-receiver*, made to take the combings from long hair—the bob did not come in until 1918. They were usually decorative and sometimes valuable and often matched the other bureau items. The most familiar were of glass, sometimes cut glass, with silver lids with small holes into which the combings could be poked; some were of china, hand-painted in the mode of the day. These, along with the round powder boxes for face powder and puffs, are big items in the antiques shops today. Some very fine varieties of glass such as wavecrest, cranberry (*see* Chapter 4), or other art glass can be found in them.

A little novelty called a *ring tree* was part of the bureau equipment along with the boxes and bottles. It was fashioned like a small branch of a tree on which milady hung her rings at night. They were usually of china, sometimes hand-painted, occasionally of silver. They are still common enough in the antiques shops and can be picked up for less than $5. Women like to buy these trees to keep on bathroom shelves or in the kitchen, so that they can park their rings when their hands go into water. As antiques they are not particularly valuable, but they are interesting and useful.

One of the relics of the past that interests collectors today is *hatpins*. In a day when hair was dressed high in pompadours, and when the wide-brimmed hats had no clips to anchor them, hatpins were necessary, and long murderous ones at that. The hatpin made a favorite gift. If you yearn to collect them you will have a wide choice. They were made of many things: silver, gold, copper, crystal, semiprecious stones, ivory, pearl, shell, agate, jade, jet. In fact, they reflected many of the styles in glass and china of the period, even to Satsuma, carnival glass, and hand-painted china. You will have a good time looking for them. They are not too expensive; good ones can be bought for $1, although unusual ones of valuable material will cost more. And, of course, you will want some of the *hatpin holders* in which the ladies used to store the long pins. They were tall, vase-like receptacles, with holes in the top, and, like the pins, they were made of the fashionable glass and china of the period. Some were fashioned to hang on the wall like small pockets. Collecting these will take a little more money than you'll need for the hatpins.

If you are looking for something to collect, dressing accessory items provide you with an area rich in possibilities, useful, amusing, and sometimes valuable. Just read the ads in a current antiques magazine and you will be amazed at the things for which there is a market: curling irons, traveler's soap dishes, mustache curlers, shoe horns, boxes used for the separate collars and cuffs before the attached ones came in, glove boxes. But as antiques of long and lasting value, they seldom have much to recommend them.

Lighting

Aside from the Tiffany-type chandeliers and table lamps of leaded glass and the art-glass shades for both gas and electric fixtures (*see* Chapters 3 and 4), there was little in the area of lighting equipment to lure the collector or tempt the antiques enthusiast in the period following 1900. A few things have ended up in the antiques shops, however, some worth buying and putting to use. There are the old *street lights,* for instance. Many of the gas lamps survived the 1900's before large arc lamps put them entirely out of use and retired the lamp lighter who went about at night with his taper. They can still be found —though not in great numbers any more—and make splendid post lanterns for both old and new houses. They are even being reproduced and used as patterns for new lanterns. If you can find one with its original iron standard, you can count yourself lucky. Many are being brought over from England and the continent, probably from the smaller towns or cities that were late in changing to modern lighting. They are easily electrified and prove very handsome when their copper and iron frames are cleaned up. If you are looking for such a lantern you can get one already finished for around $75, or in the rough for $30 to $35. But it will cost close to $30 to replace any broken glass, to burnish the copper, convert to electricity, and perhaps to provide a pole if there is none. But whichever way you chose to acquire a genuine old street lamp, the result is much more satisfactory than simply buying a brand-new one.

While you are looking you will find many other *lanterns* that were in use in the early years of the 1900's, such things as barn lanterns, railroad lanterns, police lanterns, and ship's lanterns, all of which can be turned into useful outdoor lights. If the name of Dietz, an old firm but still in business, is on such an old lantern, it becomes a preferred item. If you cannot afford or find the fine old carriage lanterns perhaps fifty years older, you can make do with an old auto lamp, the kind that used acetylene. These look like smaller versions of the carriage lamps, sometimes of brass and sometimes painted black. In pairs they make effective door lights. A pair in good condition will cost from $25 to $50. Even the small bicycle lamp that burned kerosene has its uses. They can be electrified for small night lights if you want a touch of the quaint in your home.

Another group of collectibles that are not antique, just old, are the early *light bulbs*. Many men are interested in them and look for the very old ones through which they can trace the development of electric lighting.

Automobile Items

You are not going out to buy a vintage auto unless you belong to that special dedicated group of old-car buffs. This is an expensive hobby. But you might enjoy collecting the things that went with autos in their early years; many people today buy anything that has to do with old cars, perhaps as a nostalgic gesture toward the times when roads were dusty and speed limits were not defined. Old auto costumes are amusing today, the caps and dusters, the goggles and gauntlet gloves. Your own attic may still have them in hiding. They make fine additions to the costume closet for little-theater productions or for dressing up the participants in parades of old cars.

Many shops advertise other old auto items, which usually find buyers. Besides the lamps and horns, there are the flower vases that adorned the interior of the finer cars (*see* Chapter 4), hub caps, and radiator caps. There is an active trade in old auto licenses; also in the personal license tags once issued to drivers of trucks or other commercial cars. Don't overlook old travel guides. You'll find them very interesting and perhaps amusing when compared with the new ones. Old catalogs and books of instruction appeal to some collectors even if they do not possess an old car.

All of these things are hardly antique, and certainly have little claim to quality, beauty, or promise of longevity, except as they may be bought for display in museums, like old bicycles. But they do have a ready market as part of the stock of many antiques shops, and at antiques sales. They are not particularly cheap. A license plate from 1910 on to the '20s will cost $4 or $5: a radiator cap about $8; a horn as much as $30. At least the collectors and traders have a fine time searching for old automobiliana, as well as all the other nostalgia collectibles that are around and desired today.

CHAPTER 8

FADS OF THE TIMES

JUST as they do today, the novelty makers and advertisers of the early 1900's seized on celebrities, events, and fads that took the popular fancy of the times to produce items that the public would buy in quantity. You have read (Chapter 5) how a popular magazine feature, the Gibson Girl, was immortalized by Royal Doulton on plates as well as on many other items. The Kewpies and Billiken figures are well-known examples of the way that manufacturers cashed in on a popular fancy. The Campbell's Soup Babies, modeled after the "babies" shown in the advertising displays of that company, became popular dolls. There were many more such fads. If you decide to collect in this area, remember that most of these things are valuable only as they express the tastes of the times or fill in the continuity of collections of some sort, such as dolls, china, silver.

In this category are the *Brownie items,* all taken from a series of little characters drawn by Palmer Cox for children's books. Cox's creation is important because it actually added a new member to the hierarchy of goblins and elves, as well as a new word to the dictionary. The brownie was a mischievous little spirit who came out of hiding at night to do the leftover work from the day and thus please his human supporters. He was brown in hair and complexion because he was supposed to have weathered all kinds of climate and conditions. His creator, Palmer Cox, born in Quebec in 1840, lived to see his little characters accepted by several generations of children before he died in 1924. But it is doubtful that he ever dreamed that his little elf, derived from old Scottish and German fairy legends, would become the objective of antiques collectors.

Brownie figures appeared on many china pieces, especially on those for children; as dolls (*see* rag dolls in Chapter 6), figurines of clay and plaster, cut-outs, pencils, games, spoons, souvenirs, penwipers, and a variety of other items. There were at least forty brownie characters to call on. Until the arrival of the gremlin in World War II, the brownie had things pretty much to himself as a favorite elfin symbol.

Another popular collectible that keeps many people busy searching is the *Sunbonnet Baby.* Perhaps you have seen these little figures used on china as decorations, or in prints, or books, and did not know what they were or that they are avidly collected. The little faceless child figures with big bonnets and long skirts, shown in profile, have a certain naive appeal. They were the work of a young artist, Bertha L. Corbett, who drew them almost as a joke to prove that a figure did not have to have a face to express character. Eventually

they were publicized in a small book called *Sunbonnet Babies,*
put out in 1900, with a text by Eulalie Osgood Grover.

Later, Bertha Corbett did a series of oil paintings showing
the babies at work, one for each day of the week. They became
so popular that they were used by the advertisers for many
items, all of which are collected today. They appeared on
quilts, paper dolls, Christmas cards, and Valentines. German
factories, especially Bayreuth, adopted them for use as decoration on their china. Few of the Sunbonnet Baby items would
be especially valuable if it were not for the high favor given
them by collectors. This fad is one that thrives on the fact that
the items will never be made again—except in reproduction.
Prices on the china pieces, which are more easily found than
some of the other items, sell at about the same prices as many
varieties of fine china. Buy them if you like them, but don't
take them too seriously as antiques.

The comic strips of the early 1900's produced some characters that were used in many other ways, the results of which
collectors like to buy today. *Buster Brown* with his dog, Tige,
was the first comic strip to appear in the papers. He was the
brain child of R. F. Outcault, and his appearance in the comic
supplements inspired a whole fashion of dress for children of
the time. The Buster Brown collars survived for many years;
the shoes of a company by that name still sell today. But it
was the products of at least ninety-four factories, which the
artist licensed to use Buster Brown's name, that are more apt
to attract the collector. There were Buster Brown banks, china,
figures, textiles, cigars, among other items. Interested buyers
acquire everything they can find with the name or picture of
Buster Brown. They scour the shops and read the ads for their
favorite little figure. There is even an association of Buster
Brown Comics in New York that advertises for Buster Brown

items. Other comic-paper characters followed the trend and were picked up by the novelty makers of the time, but Buster led the procession then and now. Again, collect them if you like them, but think of this as a hobby, a fun collection, rather than one of genuine value.

In the category of fads of the early 1900's are the pieces left over from the popular *home crafts* of the period. Some were pretty awful, even when technique was good. There was pyrography, a 1902 revival of an old craft called poker-painting. It consisted of burning a picture or design on leather, plush, or wood, with a red-hot platinum point kept glowing by gas pumped to the tip. Pyrography sets were sold all over the country, the cheapest costing about $2.50. Pieces could be bought already printed with a design for the amateur to follow. Decorative plaques were favorites, with the Gibson Girls and Indians taking the lead. Sometimes they were studded with glass "gems." Other pieces, sold in the art shops and department stores, to be decorated with the hot needle, included screens, picture frames, chests, stools, taborets (low stands), mirrors, lamps, book ends, umbrella stands, and even chairs and tables. This vogue lasted until 1910, when the ladies tired of it and went on to something else. Pieces decorated this way show up in the secondhand and antiques shops today. If you want to create the feeling of the turn of the century in decorating, you may want to buy them, but generally it would be no loss to the antiques field today if all examples of these burnt offerings disappeared into the limbo of old and forgotten fads. Burnt-wood novelties recently advertised included a tie rack for $4.25 and a carved wood plaque for $6, so apparently somebody buys them.

Another turn-of-the-century fad was the making of things with cigar bands. If you examine carefully the labels and cigar bands of old varieties today, you will find some interesting examples of good design. I have seen some among them good enough to be framed. But the things the ladies of the period did with them did not amount to much. They were usually pasted on pieces of china or glass to make ash trays, vases, and other knickknacks. Oh yes, you'll meet them in the shops among the antiques, but they have little aesthetic value. It was just another way in which women killed time quietly at home before the movies took them out of it and television put them back into it again.

A pastime from which relics still show up today was that of making paper "beads," by rolling strips of stiff paper over a matchstick. The paper was usually cut from a bright magazine cover in the shape of an elipse with pointed ends, which, when rolled, resulted in an oval bead, with a hole in the center for threading; the whole was then varnished. They were used for necklaces, but more often for some of the bead portieres that screened archways in halls and living rooms.

A very amusing piece, good for a laugh if you find one and recognize what it is, is an "everything jar." My mother-in-law had one and I spent hours trying to count the bits and pieces that were used in making it. Any old crock or jar was first covered with cement and then a variety of oddments were pressed into it. You could use old keys, buttons, marbles, pieces of chain, nails, screws, and broken bits of china or colored glass. The result was a sort of way-out mosaic that could easily take its place in a modern exhibit of pop art. Sometimes it ended up as a jardiniere or umbrella stand, but usually it just sat as evidence of patience and thrift with a certain pretense toward the housewife's idea of art.

It may seem out of place to mention all these things in the same book with antiques-to-be. My only reason for doing so is that they often appear in the shops that sell antiques and for that reason can be mistakenly evaluated by the casual buyer. If they appeal to you for some reason, because they are amusing, or because they tell the story of public taste at the turn of the century, or are occasionally usable, buy them. But don't think you are acquiring a new antique.

CHAPTER 9

SOUVENIR AND
COMMEMORATIVE PIECES

ALL through the history of antiques, you will find many articles in glass, pottery, china, and metal that were made expressly to commemorate an occasion or place. Classic examples are the presentation goblets of Amelung glass (one of the earliest types of fine American glass made in Maryland), souvenir boxes of Battersea enamels in England, or Leeds china pieces inscribed as souvenirs of certain English towns. These are worth a good deal, their individual values depending upon who created them, their age, and places of origin. Many souvenir pieces have been made by recognized artists. In this class of "new antiques" one can afford to look for quality because you can find many good items made in recognizable materials among the souvenir pieces, even as late as 1900 and later. Take the nine-inch bottle of milk glass (white opaque) impressed with the date and place of the New York

World's Fair of 1939. It is good enough to add to any collection of milk glass and will cost only about $5.

Fairs and exhibitions always bring out some souvenirs of lasting quality. The Centennial Exposition in Philadelphia in 1876 was the source of many things that we call antiques today. Pieces of pressed glass, such as Gillinder's famous lion glass paperweight, were made and distributed for the visitors to take home. The fairs of the later 1800's and 1900's also had their mementoes, which are being collected today. Usually they are marked in some way with the date and occasion. You will find things from the Columbian Exposition of Chicago, in 1893; the Pan-American Exposition in Buffalo, in 1901; the Louisiana Purchase Exposition, in St. Louis, in 1904; the Panama-Pacific of San Francisco, in 1915; the Sesqui-Centennial of Philadelphia, of 1926; all the way up to the Century of Progress in Chicago, in 1933; the Golden Gate International Exposition in San Francisco, in 1939; the New York World's Fair of 1939; the Seattle fair of 1962; and the New York World's Fair of 1964–1965. Items from certain fairs are not so numerous as from others, but they are around waiting to be discovered—china and glass pieces, bottles, woven silk pictures, bookmarks, toys, handkerchiefs, banks, and, currently, the little replica of the famous Pieta from the Vatican Exhibit of the New York World's Fair of 1964–1965. It will someday become an antique.

Spoons are the most common of all souvenir pieces (*see* photo section for examples). While they were popular from 1880 on, the Columbian Exposition of Chicago, in 1893, gave the spoon fad its biggest boost. Spoons have retained their popularity to this very day, and new series are being issued almost continually. If you decide to collect spoons, you should give the subject lengthy study, for they break into many groups

according to time, place, kind, and subject, and can easily
bewilder you. It is best to narrow your collecting to one classi-
fication. The Fair and Exposition spoons are only one category
(but an important one). Cities have brought out spoons for the
centennials of their foundings. Important historic events are
commemorated by spoons: the landing of the Pilgrims, the
Boston Tea Party, the sinking of the *Maine,* Columbus' discovery of America (issued in Chicago, 1893, and costing about
$7). There are spoons featuring designs of such buildings as
Faneuil Hall, Independence Hall, the Capitol Building in
Washington, D.C. Some spoons celebrate well-known places,
such as Niagara (the Niagara Indian Maiden spoon—$5), the
Golden Gate, Pike's Peak, Fujiyama, Lookout Mountain,
Monaco, Washington's Tomb, Mount Vernon (about $5) ap-
peal to some spoon collectors. There is a series of Presidential
spoons that many seek to complete. Many colleges have been
commemorated on spoons, as are the states of the union, with
their state flowers or other symbols. There are Christmas
spoons, Indian spoons, Hawaiian spoons, and a series of twelve
zodiac spoons (about $7 each), probably a birthday gift item.
These are only a few; the variety is endless. There are enough
spoons around for everybody, but certain ones are rare and
hard to come by. Advanced collectors pounce on such things
as the rare and beautifully crafted Yellowstone Elk and Bear
spoon, which may cost $9.50. Others will give thanks when
they pick up an Actor's Fund spoon showing the portraits of
five early American Theatre personages, which might cost as
much as $16. You can always find souvenir spoons at the an-
tiques shows. The cheapest will run about $1.75 to $2, for
those of no particular significance. These are the ones women
collect for use as demitasse spoons. Prices for spoons have risen
in the last few years, but one can still make up an interesting

collection in any of the categories mentioned for an average of $5 apiece.

Many collectors like spoons because of their size; most of them are made in the small demitasse size, and even larger ones do not come up to full teaspoon size. They are made of sterling, silver plate (sometimes gold-washed), gold, and copper. The finest, especially those from foreign countries, are enameled. Some of the Russian enameled spoons are exquisite. A trip around the world can be recorded in spoons of real worth. Decorations are often on the back of the bowls as well as on the tip and front of the handles. They can be displayed in many interesting ways: in racks, in frames, on tray tables under glass, or kept in velvet-lined drawers—another use for the spool cabinet (*see* Chapter 7).

This "new antique" has inherent quality. Spoons show great ingenuity and fine craftsmanship (though they seldom, if ever, are accredited to any one maker), and are one of the best areas to investigate if you want to go collecting in the "new antiques" market.

Souvenir *handkerchiefs* have always been a collectible item. The most valuable from the antiques viewpoint are those early large printed squares of silk or cotton put out in the 1700's and early 1800's. Most of them commemorate some historical event or personage. Washington, the favorite, appears on such handkerchiefs in many guises. These are for advanced collectors and museums. But the idea of recording some noteworthy event in a printed picture on silk or cotton has kept on, and it is possible to find late examples of such souvenirs. They include the publicized campaigns of Presidents Cleveland, McKinley, and Theodore Roosevelt, and expositions as late as the New York World's Fair of 1939, which commemorated its Pavilion of Nations in this fashion. If you are interested in handkerchief collecting, begin with the more recent ones and work back toward the older and rarer ones.

I have mentioned recent examples of glass souvenirs (*see* Chapter 4), also china novelties, dolls, and paperweights. Each has its place in the picture of late antiques, some good, some not so good. But of them all, among the most interesting and rewarding to the collector, are commemorative *plates*. For reasonably inexpensive collecting and an investment for tomorrow, those made just before and continuing after 1900 are ideal. Use of American historic scenes and events on china was commercialized by the English Staffordshire potters in the early 1800's for the American trade. These plates in rich cobalt blue—sometimes flowing blue—are what is called Historic Blue in the roster of early antiques. They are becoming prohibitive in price because they have been so assiduously collected for years, but later plates made by both English and American firms will fit into almost any collector's budget. One of the most prolific potters of these later plates was Wedgwood. These picture plates that began coming over around the turn of the century and continue right up to today, are called Late Wedgwood and can be bought for $5 or $6. They include such subjects as Faneuil Hall, the Boston State House, Mount Vernon, the Public Library in Boston, the Library of Congress, and many places not so easily recognizable. The quality and printing is good, as would be expected of anything bearing the Wedgwood imprint. They sell for about $6 apiece. Rowland and Marcellus is an important mark to look for in this group.

The popularity of these imported commemorative plates stirred our American firms into marketing similar ones. Jones, McDuffee and Straton, of Boston; and Wright, Tyndale and Van Roden, of Philadelphia, appear on plates made much like those of the Staffordshire potters. They were *not* reproductions, in spite of their close resemblance. Nobody has ever been able to duplicate the old deep blue of the early Staffordshire plates, but the American ones were designed by good artists or transfers printed from good sources.

American factories that put out historical plates included the Mercer Pottery Company of Trenton whose Penn plate, issued in 1901, is a classic. The American plates featured many subjects similar to those shown by Wedgwood, and in addition you can find such specialties as the plates showing the Brooklyn Bridge, made for the tercentenary of Long Island, the design taken from a lithograph by Joseph Pennell. Since many issues of centennial and commemorative plates, whether for towns, colleges, or events, were limited in number, they are harder to come by for collecting and, therefore, more important. You can't go wrong in buying them, even if they have no special interest for you. The current ones undoubtedly will be antiques someday.

In line with these souvenir items is a more specialized group —*coronation pieces*. Inasmuch as we have always welcomed ceramic pieces from England, these should appeal to American collectors. There are enough of them to prove interesting and valuable, too. The earliest and rarest start with the blue-dash chargers of English delft, from the reigns of Charles I and William III, in the 1600's, and go right through to the Victorian period. But the 1900's have not been without them. You will find pieces put out to celebrate the accessions of later monarchs, Edward VII, George V, Edward VIII, George VI, and Elizabeth II. Although the reign of Edward, the Prince of Wales, who abdicated, lasted for such a short period, many souvenir pieces were issued for it; today these have special value because of their rarity and perhaps because of sentiment toward the young king who gave up his throne for "the woman he loved." They, too, are antiques of the future. Because of this I was surprised to find such a commemorative mug in a dusty little antiques shop in Maryland one day. It lay among a lot of junk and odds and ends priced at $1. It showed the picture of Edward VIII and the date of his accession to the throne. It was not of particularly fine china, just a cheap souvenir piece, but I snapped it up because I knew that someday it would be valuable. I see more of these pieces around now that people are aware of their value as commemorative antiques.

Another commemorative group are the items having to do with our presidents of the last seventy-five years. There have been thirteen of them, from Benjamin Harrison on. Many of the presidents have been remembered in plates, and if you collect them you should try to fill out the series if you can. Portraits as well as birthplaces of some presidents have been pictured on china for the most part, but some pieces in glass were inspired by the chief executives of a period, such as the McKinley campaign plates of 1896, put out by McKee and Brothers, and the Garfield memorial plate (1881).

Still another grouping in this commemorative and souvenir list are the *fraternal-order items* of the early 1900's. These are mostly Masonic, although I have an Elk plate of the B.P.O.E. done in the "new tole" in metal (*see* Chapter 7). If your preference for Masonic items starts you collecting or if you want something unusual to give to a relative or friend who is a Mason, you won't have too much trouble finding china or glass marked with Masonic emblems. These were usually souvenirs of conventions or of local celebrations of lodges or commanderies. Your choice is wide; you can find tumblers, goblets, spooners, plates, cups and saucers, shaving mugs, paperweights, etc. The glass is usually pressed, sometimes colored, as in the Masonic flasks of an earlier period (up to 1830 and revived later). China is transfer-printed. All show Masonic symbols and usually the date and nature of the event. It is an interesting area to explore. Items are not too rare nor are they common, but they, like other commemorative pieces, were limited in number. Prices are not high, seldom over $15 for a single piece.

If you want to know where to find any of these special items mentioned in these last three chapters, or in fact any of the late antiques, you have several sources. The most logical and commonest way is to go through the shops or exhibits at antiques shows; or you may elect to dig through the secondhand shops or junk outlets; you can attend sales, not passing up the smaller country sales; or you could read the ads in the antiques magazines, where dealers from all over the country publicize their mail-order businesses. You can scan the ads of individuals in your local newspaper, or keep an eye on the old houses in your neighborhood, where, occasionally, the older members of a family may be ready to sell out; if you are known to them, you may be able to buy certain pieces before the antiques dealers beat you to it. Both friendship and contacts count in this business of tracing antiques. People are more apt to sell to an individual than to a dealer. The old antagonism toward dealers as "gyps" is still more generally held than you would suppose. Sometimes the reputation was earned, but I would say that today the majority of dealers are honest and reasonable in their dealings with the public.

Always ask *first* what the owner of an antique piece wants for it. This is even required by law in some states. Usually he says he doesn't know. Perhaps he doesn't, but perhaps he is afraid to commit himself, hoping you will offer more. Then it is up to you to make him an offer fair enough to quiet your conscience and in line with what a dealer would offer. You have to know the market to do this in honesty. The least you can do is to offer what the piece is worth to you. I feel it is best to stick to your offer. Don't play hot and cold with the seller. If you keep on raising the price of your offer, he gets suspicious and will often refuse to sell—and with good reason. He will argue that if the piece was worth that, why didn't you offer it in the first place, and that you are no better than the dealers.

An individual who has been collecting, as well as a good dealer, knows what he *ought* to pay for a piece, and if he doesn't offer that in the beginning he deserves to lose out. Of course, the antiques business is built up on canny buying, and the argument is that if the seller is satisfied, why worry. The specialized knowledge of a dealer or individual buyer should stand him in good stead in looking for "sleepers" in a shop, at a sale, or in an old house. To many a householder, a lot of what he or she wants to get rid of is simply junk, and he is inclined to let it go inexpensively just to get rid of it. This is how a lot of these late antiques have come on the market.

There is a wonderful story going around right now—and it is all true, as I have had a chance to prove. A farmer bought a box of "junk" at a country sale for fifty cents; going through his prize package, he found a small pewter communion flagon that meant nothing to him. But another bidder at the same sale happened to see and handle it, and recognized the initials on it, *I C H,* as those of Johann Christopher Heyne, of Lancaster, Pennsylvania, one of the earliest pewterers of America. Not to let it get away, he offered the farmer $400 for it. The man took it gratefully. It was a very fair offer. The buyer might have gotten it for $4, but he knew he could afford the

$400, for he also knew, because of his specialized knowledge of old pewter, that he stood to make a good profit on it. He later sold it for a profit, and it was then resold—finally for $5000. It will end up—if it hasn't already—as a museum piece. This is a good example of the way antiques reach their peak in price. The farmer would never have been able to sell it for $5000. The second man had to place it where its value was known, but he was satisfied in getting a splendid profit, leaving it to a third party to cash in on it to the limit with a collector.

CHAPTER 10

SEEN IN THE SHOPS

I KNOW by this time that you, the reader, are going to ask, "But where do I find these things? Do all the antiques shops have them?" No, not *all* shops, but these late items are fairly well distributed in the antiques shops all over the country. Some dealers even specialize in them, and advertise their specialties in the antiques magazines.

There are five good sources for finding antiques. The most logical and widespread way is to visit your local antiques shops, and to stop off wherever you see the sign "Antiques" as you travel. A shopkeeper welcomes a visitor if he has a certain interest in mind, even if the dealer cannot supply it. There is a world of difference between such a visitor and the casual looker, who goes "antiquing" as a pastime or perhaps to compare prices or to learn about antiques the easiest way. Don't be a looker, or let the dealer assume you are one. You may find him brusque and impatient because he knows he is just wasting his time. Ask immediately when you go into a shop for what you want. The dealer will then be able to bring out— perhaps from a dark corner—what you could pass by in idle "looking," or suggest some other shop where you might find it.

Visit the antiques shows. Almost every town has one nowadays, sponsored by some local organization in the community. Here you have the opportunity to look over the wares of many dealers both local and from far places in one afternoon or evening. It increases your chances of finding what you want. Prices at antiques shows are apt to be a little higher than those you meet in the shops, for several reasons: the dealers usually bring their best pieces; they have expenses to meet, rental for their booths, transportation, labor, etc.; and they must price high enough to take care of the discount they will give the other dealers (with whom they do a lot of business at such shows). But it is worth paying a small premium if you find an elusive thing you have been seeking, and you will save time by covering shows.

Don't fail to look through the secondhand shops or junk outlets, rummage sales, and white elephant shops. Though they are pretty well combed by antiques dealers, it is not impossible to find something that they have passed by if you are willing to search carefully.

Attend the antiques auctions, both the smaller country sales as well as the big-city auction rooms. Many good antiques end up here, and if things are auspicious—bad weather, lack of publicity, several shows scheduled on one day—you may get good buys. But on the whole, prices tend to be high at the sales because the spirit of competition often forces them up. Don't be too impulsive and overbid. Wait, rather than pay too much for what you want.

The individual who goes out on his own to buy antiques has one advantage over the dealer: he is not buying to sell, at least not in the near future. Generally speaking there is not much resale in these new antiques for the collector who buys at retail. It isn't likely that what you buy, except in the quality brackets of glass, china, dolls, or perhaps an unusual piece, will make you a lot of money. It is not a factor that you can count on, as you can with many older antiques that rise in price year by year. So base your buying price upon the present market, figuring that the piece you want is worth it for as long as you may want to hold on to it. If the price rises, so much the better, but don't count on its holding up. The antiques market fluctuates almost as much as the stock market. There will always be some "blue-chip" items that hold their own through any kind of a recession or when interest dies down in other faddish and less valuable items. Like stocks, some pieces are good only for a quick turnover, which is more the concern of the dealer than the individual collector. You will have to judge values for yourself by keeping your ears tuned for the changes in the market, watching the prices in the shops, and asking questions where you can. Very often the collector, who gets around to a great many shops, will know more about what is going on in his line than the dealers themselves.

Collectors are expressing interest in many things that are not primarily found among the antiques items of the shops, such as many of the *inventions* and mechanical aids to living during the early years of the century. Many of these are bought by business firms to exhibit the steps in the development of their products. Many are bought by those who for one reason or another have an interest in some mechanical specialty like lawn mowers, which came into their own around 1900. These are more likely to be picked up at sales or in junk yards.

Typewriters go back as far as 1874; the first one, marketed by Remington, had only capital letters. Since then improvements have been made over the years, resulting in a great variety of models for the interested collector to seek.

The *cash register* was a turn-of-the-century invention. It was a big boon to the storekeeper of the late 1890's. Like the typewriter, its development provides the collector with a variety of models to search for as they are discarded from old stores and business establishments. They seldom make the antiques shops, but appear when there is a sale of old equipment.

In 1900 nobody had an electric refrigerator. The old zinc-lined *ice box* was the rule. It was usually of oak, and was sometimes prettied up with a mirror or an additional cupboard, and it often took its place as a piece of furniture in the dining room. People are buying them today to turn into radio or TV cabinets. They have no particular quality, but they make conversation pieces for the recreation room, or beside the barbecue, for actual use as a container in which to chill bottles. You should be able to pick one up for a couple of dollars.

There were no electric *washing machines* before 1920, when the first Maytag washer came into use. There is not much one can do with an old washing machine except perhaps fill it with plants on a terrace or patio. But commercial firms concerned with the laundry business often buy them up for display, as they do the old pressing irons, washboards, and pleating irons.

Vacuum sweepers were well on their way by 1920, the carpet sweeper preceding them in 1916. Most of the old sweepers have been traded in on new models. Where do they end up? It is hard to say, but undoubtedly some have fallen into the hands of collectors who have an interest in tracing the development of this household item that progressed so quickly from a luxury to a necessity.

Telephones were, of course, in use at the end of the century, and I have mentioned the wall phones and the foreign phones so popular in the antiques shops now. The tall phones on a standard, which replaced the wall phone, have also passed into the limbo of antiques. They are being bought up for lamp bases; many shops sell them already converted into lamps. These novelties are not common enough to have a set price.

Aside from these inventions or improvements, there are a number of peculiar items, some scarcely fifty years old, appearing among the antiques in the shops and in the secondhand and junk shops. One thing about them is sure—they will never appear any more and perhaps that makes them eligible for collecting. For example, it seems unlikely that anyone would ever want an old peanut-vending machine with its piping steam whistle from its roaster. Yet at least one—and maybe more—imaginative buyer has put one to use in her game room as a serving cart. It makes an amusing piece. So do the merry-go-round animals widely sought for game rooms. These pieces, however, are not cheap. One can pay $250 or more for a realistic horse, pig, or lion. The reason is that they have come to be recognized as examples of primitive art and are being sold by dealers who specialize in things like store signs, wooden Indians, and such. Would you recognize a "busybody" if you saw one? Probably not unless you had lived in Baltimore or Philadelphia where they were common. It is a pair of mirrors used outside an upper window (particularly on the characteristic row house), angled so that from upstairs one could see who was standing at the front door. It saved the housewife many steps and was an easy way to get rid of beggars, solicitors, and unwanted callers. I often wonder what has become of them. I have seen only a few around, but I am sure a busybody could be put to some use today, and would prove an investment as well as antique from the turn of the century.

Bells are a great favorite with collectors, but in this particular antiques period not many were developed that were different enough to be collectible. One was the trolley bell, of brass or iron, with a cord to pull and operate the gong. These make fine doorbells. There are also the jingling store bells that worked on metal springs over the door. Men look for old fire-engine bells and locomotive bells that were in use after 1900.

Parasols did not go out as a fashionable item until 1915, which leaves many still in the stores today. Often, though the silk or lace is in bad condition, the frames and handles are good. There are people who collect umbrella and parasol handles, and the results are usually interesting if they include carved wood, metals, porcelain, and other materials. Parasols have their use in a costume closet for masquerades or amateur theater productions.

Opera glasses from this period are also a desirable collectible to be found in antiques shops. They were usually made in France and were quite elegant, with mother-of-pearl embellishments. Some were handled like lorgnettes. Few people use them today. They are luxury items to be gathered up as a record of a more elegant way of life.

You could join those who are collecting old candy and ice-cream *molds* of tin and pewter and find this hobby inexpensive and rewarding. There are many small, two-part, hinged molds of pewter to be found, used usually for shaping chocolate candies. Subjects include bunnies, Santa Clauses, roses, turkeys, fish, hearts, ears of corn, a clasped hand. They are not costly, prices running from five to eight or nine dollars. These may also have been used for ice cream, though molds once used in the corner bakery that made its own ice cream are apt to be larger. They make decorative pieces for a kitchen shelf or cupboard.

Doorstops offer an interesting variety for collecting or for use. All sorts of heavy objects were used for this purpose. Some women even worked petit-point covers for bricks, but most were of iron or brass. Animals, such as cats, dogs, lions, foxes, and frogs, seemed to be favored, and were used from the late Victorian period up to about 1920. A bulldog of iron, usually painted realistically, is something you will see in many shops for about $6. Occasionally, you can also find the old hitching weights of stone or iron that were used to keep horses from wandering away with the buggies. They'll keep a door open against the strongest wind.

Pillow shams, those squares of embroidered or ruffled linen used to cover the pillows of a bed in the daytime, have takers in the shops. For anyone determined to give an antique bed a truly old-time look, these provide very effective accents. Along with them you can find Marseilles spreads, which were woven white cotton coverlets with a rather elaborate pattern. They no longer look old-fashioned, only interesting and practical when used today. Some were very heavy and as handsome as fine damask. They sell today for $8 up. They take a dye very nicely if you want to color them, and can even be divided and used as draperies.

Men still shaved at home as the years turned the century, using the old-fashioned open-blade razor, which they sharpened on a leather strop—a handy thing to use for spanking, by the way. The safety razor did not come in until 1913. There is enough variety in old *razors* to encourage collecting. The men in your family might particularly enjoy hunting for them, just the way many men seek out old cigar cutters, mustache cups, and pocket flasks of the period.

High in favor among many collectors are *Christmas-tree ornaments*. The Christmas tree was not adopted as a custom in this country until the middle of the 1800's. It was originally a German custom, but was sponsored by Queen Victoria, and welcomed over here by our German immigrants. The first trees had homemade trimmings, popcorn, cranberry chains, gingerbread figures, and marzipan sweets. The first balls, or "baubles," as they were called, came from the Thuringia forest area of Germany. Up until World War I most of our tree ornaments were imported from Germany, and it is these that you should search for if you want to collect in this area. There are not many around because the blown glass balls and figures were fragile, but little tinsel angels, paper dolls, stars, icicles, and figures survive. So do the small clip-on candle holders that became useless when candles were outlawed as tree lighting because of fire hazards. Too bad. There was an indescribable scent to Christmas morning when the folding doors to the front parlor were opened and a potpourri of burning wax, pine needles, and fresh glue from the doll's house came pouring out. It will never come again. There is no magic moment of unveiling now that trees are trimmed days ahead and the children are allowed to help. One of the best ways to recapture that old feeling is to cherish the ornaments that may have come down to you from generations past. Next best, go out and buy whatever lovely old ones that you can find in the shops.

Napkin rings were a Victorian nicety when one used a napkin over again for several meals. They were still used after 1900, until disposable napkins came in, or at least until home laundering became easier. The fanciest rings belong to the Victorian years. These were usually of silver plate with the ring part of a composition with figures, such as birds, children, or other objects, which made them decorative pieces as well as useful. Those made later, in the early 1900's, were plain silver bands, perhaps etched or decorated like any silver table piece, often with the name or monogram included. Such silver rings, when cut apart by your jeweler to insert a clasp, make attractive bracelets. Some napkin rings were made in cut glass.

The tea table still had a place in the parlor at the turn of the century. It was equipped with the fine china of the day, often with cups and saucers that were one of a kind and collected for that purpose. The "company" *tea sets* were usually of plated silver. Also there was usually a spirit-burning lamp on the table, on which the tea *kettle* of hot water could be kept boiling. You can find these graceful little brass or silver kettles on their metal stands today; they are very useful for making instant coffee or tea at the table. They run about $17 to $20.

CHAPTER 11

ANTIQUES OF THE FUTURE

IN considering the antiques of this century it might be well to look ahead as well as backward. Many things being made today will be worth the name of antique in a few years. The keener collectors are buying them up. Take *Tobies,* those little character jugs with a history of two hundred years. Everyone who knows anything about them realizes that they are getting very expensive. Those dating back to the 1700's, to the days of Ralph Wood, Whieldon, Pratt, and many other Staffordshire makers, can bring as much as $200, but good jugs are being made today. Many commemorate people in the news, such as Churchill, MacArthur, Eisenhower, and so on. Most of them are English, a few are French. The Japanese are making them, too, sometimes fairly good ones. Visitors to the British Isles and Canada often bring home modern Toby jugs made by English potters, especially Doulton, which makes so many fine modern figurines. They are cheaper to buy in Europe because, as gifts or souvenirs costing less than $10, they can be sent home duty-free. But the new Tobies found here in the shops are not particularly cheap. They will run about $10 or $20, and many resembling the old ones—and sometimes passed off as old—will cost in the neighborhood of $50. But they are worth storing up against the future if you have missed out on the old ones when they were more available.

Another modern ceramic that many of us have been collecting for the last ten or fifteen years is the appealing little *Hummel figures*. These were originally the work of a German Franciscan nun, named Sister H. Innocentia, born Berta Hummel in 1909. As a young girl she had studied art in Munich, but in 1934 she gave up the life of the world and retired to the convent. Her artistic skill persisted, and she began to create naive, innocent child figurines that proved marketable and provided funds for her sisterhood. She captured the simplicity and appeal of the children she had known as a child herself, showing them at work and at play. There are about 150 different subjects, not counting the madonnas, angels, and crêche figures, all signed Hummel. Sister Innocentia died in 1946, but the figures continued to be put out by a licensed German firm and are so signed. They are a great favorite with travelers to Germany today and are sold in this country in the better gift shops. All genuine Hummel figures must be marked with the name H. I. Hummel, and are not inexpensive. Of course, there are many reproductions, even Japanese, that superficially resemble the original ones. But only the signed Hummels are worth buying to enjoy now and to save for the years to come. They have the quality that makes for a true antique.

I am almost afraid to mention the *Doughty birds* (*see* photo section) because they have risen to prices so high that they are nearly unattainable. One could buy a good car for what one would have to pay for one of these beautiful porcelain pieces today, and not many of us are prepared to do that, even as an investment opportunity. Still they are proof of one thing: a piece of porcelain does not have to be as old as Meissen, Bow, or Capo-di-Monte to bring a top price. They were created by Dorothy Doughty, an English artist, in her Cornwall studio, for the Royal Worcester works. They were designed with such skill and verisimilitude that they stand far out in the works of art of this century. Dorothy Doughty sketched her birds in their native habitats, and usually made them in pairs, as did Audubon in his paintings before her. Her production was always limited, the editions never running more than five hundred of a kind. This accounts for the high prices as much as does the artistry of the figures. Perhaps one element contributing to their popularity is their faithfulness to real birds. People understand them and find them familiar and appealing. From 1935 to 1960 this artist created about thirty subjects. Her career came to an end with her death three years ago. While most of us can never hope to own a Doughty bird, it is a good thing to be able to recognize one when we see it in a collection or in a shop, to appreciate its beautiful porcelain texture, its exquisite coloring, its imaginative grouping, and the sharp modeling in a figure that is often no more than nine inches high.

Another artist of note, an American, Edward M. Biehm, creates exquisite porcelain bird figures in his studio in Washington's Crossing, Pennsylvania. His work carries on the Doughty tradition, and his creations are becoming almost as hard to track down. When you do find them the prices now will astound you, going into the thousands. Anyone who was wise enough to have bought them about fifteen years ago could have got them at fairly reasonable prices, perhaps as low as $100. Moral: get in at the beginning, when you discover something worthwhile.

In the same class of the almost unattainable, sure to be worth more, are the extraordinary display pieces of *contemporary Steuben glass*—bowls, vases, and other decorative items. These massive moldings of brilliant clear glass are engraved with a variety of designs. Each is a triumph of a modern designer's art. They are widely advertised at prices running well into the hundreds, so someone is buying them. They are favorite gifts by the government to foreign officials, distinctive expressions of the best in American art. But cheer up! I have just seen a beautiful small Steuben glass bowl marked only $25, so there is hope that some of us can possess pieces of this fine glassware built for a long life and slated for fame.

Grandma Moses oils have now moved into the top-gallery bracket. But before the public began to appreciate this unusually gifted and untutored painter of modern primitives, one could have acquired a Grandma Moses scene for well under $500. Of course, now that she has died—at age 100—there will be no more of her pictures, and this raises the prices even more. Still, I think if I could find the cash and the opportunity to pick up a Grandma Moses canvas at the going market price of $4,000 to $12,000, I'd do it. She will live on, if only as an inspiration to all senior citizens who would like to lead useful lives and excel at something in their later years.

A modern art glass that is showing up in the shows and shops rather regularly now is *Gundersen glass;* it so closely resembles the early Burmese and Peachblow (*see* Chapter 4) that it can easily be taken for it. The Gundersen Glass Company is successor to the Pairpont Company, which was formerly the Mt. Washington Glass Company, producer of some of the finest art glass of the 1880's and 1890's. The shapes of the Gundersen pieces are very similar to the early ones, and the colors, shading from opaque white, or cream, to rose, are good, though professionals say not as good as in the early glass. It is a heavy, acid (dull) glass and has enough quality to carry it along through the years to the status of the best antiques. While not quite as expensive as the early Burmese or Peachblow, it costs plenty, but is worth it. A recent ad in one of the antiques magazines offered a Gundersen cup and saucer for $125.

In the discussion of glass (Chapter 4) I mentioned the *Kasiun paperweights* that have been made in the last ten to fifteen years. Their quality rivals the best of the weights made in the 1800's, and they are not cheap. A small faceted Kaziun weight might run to $125, but in comparison with many of the French weights, such as Baccarat, St. Louis, or Clichy, they are a good buy for the collector, for they will hold up in value.

Some of the *hooked rugs* being made today are works of art. They are being designed by well-known artists, often in the most modern of designs. They are not primitive-looking, as are the old rugs, but are well done and should be worth as much to the next generation as the old Orientals are to ours. When they are executed by hand, with good designs, they qualify as true antiques-to-be.

Women are doing a lot of creative work at home today, and surely some of the *embroidery* such as crewelwork and needlepoint from their hands will live on, as will much of their handmade jewelry and ceramics. One enterprising young woman is creating original window transparencies made from old bits and pieces of colored glass that she puts together (with lead, as in church windows) into all kinds of figures, mostly modern in feeling, but of a quality that insures their life and value for many years.

The common denominator in all this modern work is that these antiques of the future are made by hand and show the skill of true artists and artisans. Undoubtedly there are many other items, handmade, or occasionally mass-produced, that show quality enough to warrant a long life in the antiques field. It requires a discerning eye to recognize and assess their worth before the stamp of public approval focuses on them and pegs up the price. But why not be the one to do the spotting yourself, and find among today's new beauties in the crafts those pieces that may turn out to be distinguished antiques of the future?

Chapter 12

ABOUT REPRODUCTIONS

Y OU cannot talk about antiques without mentioning a major threat to all collectors—the reproductions. Many are so good that they cannot be readily identified as new. These deceptive pieces haunt us all, whether we are after the genuine old things or only the later antiques of the 20th century. Reproductions present a problem you have to learn your way around, whether they are fakes made deliberately to deceive or just fine attempts to reproduce old craftsmanship. If they are sold as the real thing they can do a lot of harm, especially if prices are in line with those for originals. You are paying for age—and a certain quality—that isn't there.

One way to spot reproductions is by the price. Because they are sold wholesale in quantity, and hence fairly cheap to the retail shops, your suspicions should be aroused by finding them in the antiques shops at prices far below the market. You should also stop and think when you suddenly see a number of the same items around that are usually rather uncommon, such as blue glass hats made to hold toothpicks or matches. There are genuine old ones available, but not as many as you will see in the shops.

Although prices in the shops vary considerably with locality, turnover, and the buying wisdom of the dealer, there is no real cut-price market in antiques. Informed buyers adhere more or less to the "going price" established by an average in the market, and sometimes by published price guides (*see* Bibliography). And so, if you see a Stippled Star goblet, one of the popular patterns in pressed glass, a very lovely one with small stars on a stippled background, priced at only $3 or $4, when it should sell for $8 or $9, you should begin to wonder. Sometimes a dishonest or unknowing dealer will price a reproduction the same as he would the real thing. If in doubt, better pass it up, especially if the dealer cannot vouch for its age. Maybe he—or she—will say, "I bought it for old," or, "I don't really know, I *think* it is old," which lets him out and puts the burden of the decision on you.

Even if the reproduction is not a fake, and sold to deceive, but is openly a copy, it can still do harm in another way. It makes the genuine antique item that it imitates seem so common, so familiar, that one can lose interest in the original. I know that has happened with such popular things as Daisy and Button or Hobnail glass pieces, found now in reproduction in every gift shop. When you see these in numbers on every hand you can't care much about displaying the genuine old pieces. Reproductions thus water the market. They also make the average buyer suspicious and afraid to buy even in the better antiques shops.

Dealers will argue that good reproductions sold as such are

a boon to those who cannot afford the real thing. Young marrieds who like Early American or Victorian cannot be blamed for buying facsimiles of what they yearn to possess. On the other hand, many good reproductions cost almost as much as old pieces, especially in furniture; yet, good as they are, they are not really worth more than other well-made modern furniture. So you have to make up your mind whether to accept the new that merely looks like the old, with none of its built-in value, or go more slowly and pick up old pieces as you find them. Of course, some people do not care. All they want is the antique effect. But remember, as an investment the antiques have it all over the reproductions for resale. Ten years from now, even ten months, the reproductions will be only secondhand furniture, and your new antique, if good, well chosen, and well cared for, will mellow even more and prove an investment that has increased in value.

The minute anything in the antiques market becomes popular, someone sets out to reproduce it, if it is only a three-dollar iron trivet, match safe, or string-holder. It seems strange to me that this holds for such small items. You might expect to see fakes and reproductions of more valuable pieces where the profit is larger—pieces such as furniture, pewter, milk glass and other choice glass made in the old patterns, rare mechanical banks, copper weathervanes, Paul Revere lanterns, coach lanterns. But to have to reckon with copies of the newer things of no great value, things that many of us can remember or even still possess, seems to be carrying it too far. If these items stayed in the gift shops, I would not object. But they don't— they creep over into so-called antiques shops.

Right now, items popular for only a few years are being reproduced in quantity. You can now buy new ice-cream-parlor chairs and tables, new bentwood pieces, new brass costumers, new wicker exactly like the old. Even cut glass, supposedly irreplaceable, is being imported from Germany, I understand; I haven't seen it yet. Experts also say to beware when you are about to pay out several hundred dollars for a piece of Holly Amber (*see* Chapter 4) because it is being reproduced. I have mentioned the new metal agate ware in mottled blue and white and other colors that is being copied after the now-popular old kitchen ware that was pure junk a couple of years ago. Very ornate and handsome—and apparently old—carriage lamps that are as new as last week are coming in from Europe. European shops are overflowing with new pewter and brass and much is sent to America. I have been told that copper luster china can now be reproduced, but I haven't caught up with it yet. Many of these particular reproductions are recognizable, and, in fact, many reproductions are easily spotted if you take time to examine them. But there are many that defy the experts, despite all the information and experience they have to call on.

There are various ways to establish authenticity. Markings are usually safe, though it has been known that some of these are counterfeit. An old pewter mark, for instance, can be soldered on an unmarked piece. Old nails can be used to make a new piece made of old wood look genuine. Authorities can tell exciting stories of the lengths to which the makers of fakes and the perpetrators of deception will go to "make" an antique. But such things are the exception and need not concern the casual buyer too much; it is the more usual things you meet in the shops that may stump you. There are a few rules that may help:

Shop for a good dealer, one with a long and well-earned reputation for honesty and reliability. A dealer who guarantees his items to be old and will take back anything you may have a doubt about is to be trusted.

Try to find out the "history" of the piece, where it came from, if you can. This is where you will have to take the dealer's word.

Just because a piece is sold with a lot of other old things in a sale from an old house will not necessarily stamp it as old. It may have been a recent five-and-dime-store acquisition.

Compare, if you can, a doubtful piece with one that you know absolutely to be old. (One woman I know who collects old spatter carries a small piece with her when she goes antiquing so that she can compare pieces she sees in the shops with her own.)

Handle, feel, and weigh old pieces whenever you get the chance, to give yourself some experience to use in buying. The things that give away reproductions are size, weight, slight variations in pattern, sharp edges when they should be smooth, or vice versa, the use of colors that were never used for the old pieces, smudged painting, or lack of signs of wear.

An expert keeps all these things in mind and backs them up by keeping alert and learning about the new revealing signs appearing among the reproductions. Articles in the antiques magazines will often enlighten the reader on what is being reproduced. It all means taking a bit of trouble, but it's worth it if you don't want to be fooled.

Is there anything we can do about these out-and-out fakes as well as the innocent reproductions to offset this confusion in the antiques world? There should be a way of dating them. I am not alone in urging for some kind of legislation that will make it imperative to stamp the date of manufacture on anything—wood, metal, glass, or china—that could be mistaken for an antique. Simply changing the pattern or shape or quality will not be enough to make the fraud legal; a date would settle it for good. The McKinley Act, which required the name of the country of origin stamped or painted on every antique import from 1891 on, has helped enormously in identification. Without it one can say, fairly accurately, that a foreign piece was made before that date.

In the meantime, keep your eyes open, keep informed, and don't believe everything you see or hear. But don't stop buying. That would end all the fun.

BIBLIOGRAPHY

(NOTE: If your local book shop or library does not have these books, look among the ads of the antiques magazines, as many are privately printed, or order from Antiques Publications, Inc., Teneytown, Maryland, which carries most antiques books.)

General

ALLEN, FREDERICK LEWIS. *Only Yesterday*. New York: Harper & Row, 1931.

Antiques and Their Current Prices, 8th edition. Uniontown, Pennsylvania: E. G. Warman Publishing Company, 1965.

BEDFORD, JOHN. *Looking in Junk Shops*. New York: David McKay Company, Inc., 1964.

————. *More Looking in Junk Shops*. New York: David McKay Company, Inc., 1965.

Collectors' Guide to American Recordings, 1895–1925. New York: American Record Collectors Exchange, 1952.

GRIFFITH, F. H. *Mechanical Bank Booklet*. Pittsburgh, Pennsylvania (P.O. Box 10644): Privately printed, 1965.

HANKENSON, DICK. *Trivets*. Maple Plain, Minnesota: Privately printed, 1963.

HARDT, ANTON. *Souvenir Spoons of the 90's*. New York (335 Bleecker Street): Privately printed, 1962.

JOHNSON, LAURENCE. *Over the Counter and on the Shelf*. Rutland, Vermont: Charles E. Tuttle Company, 1961.

LEE, RUTH WEBB. *Antique Fakes and Reproductions*. Wellesley Hills, Massachusetts (105 Suffolk Road): Lee Publications, 1950.

MEBANE, JOHN. *Treasure at Home*. New York: A. S. Barnes & Co., 1964.

MILLS, JOHN FITZMAURICE. *Care of Antiques*. New York: Hastings House, 1964.

PETERSON, A. G. *Salt and Salt Shakers*. Silver Spring, Maryland (415 Pershing Drive): Privately printed, 1961.

ROGERS, AGNES. *I Remember Distinctly*. New York: Harper & Row, 1947.

SAVAGE, GEORGE. *Forgeries, Fakes, and Reproductions*. New York: Frederick A. Praeger, Inc., 1964.

SCOTT, CHRISTOPHER and AMORET. *Collecting Bygones*. New York: David McKay Company, Inc., 1965.

SHULL, THELMA. *Victorian Antiques*. Rutland, Vermont: Charles E. Tuttle Co., 1963.

Glass

HARTUNG, MARION T. *Carnival Glass*, Books I–IV. Emporia, Kansas (718 Institution Street): Privately printed, 1961.

HERRICK, RUTH. *Greentown Glass*. Grand Rapids, Michigan (26 Sheldon Avenue, S.E.): Privately printed, 1951.

HOTCHKISS, J. H. *Carder's Steuben Glass and Price Guide*. Rochester, New York (87 Sagamore Street): Privately printed, 1965.

KENDRICK, GRACE. *The Antique Bottle Collector*. Fallon, Nevada (485 West 4th Street): Privately printed, 1963.

KOCH, ROBERT. *Louis C. Tiffany: Rebel in Glass*. New York: Crown Publishers, 1964.

LAGERBURG, TED and VI. *Collectible Glass*. New Port Richey, Florida: Modern Photographers, 1963.

METZ, ALICE HULETT. *Early American Pressed Glass*. Chicago, Illinois (2004 West 102nd Street): Privately printed, 1958.

PETERSON, A. G. *333 Glass Salt Shakers*. Silver Spring, Maryland (416 Pershing Drive): Privately printed, 1965.

PRESNICK, ROSE M. *Carnival and Iridescent Glass Price Guide*. Miskell Printing Co., 1961.

PUTNAM, H. E. *Bottle Identification*. Jamestown, California: Privately printed, 1965.

REVI, ALBERT CHRISTIAN. *American Cut and Engraved Glass*. New York: Thomas Nelson and Sons, 1965.

―――. *American Pressed Glass and Figural Bottles*. New York: Thomas Nelson and Sons, 1964.

―――. *Nineteenth Century Glass*. New York: Thomas Nelson and Sons, 1959.

WATSON, RICHARD. *Bitters Bottles*. New York: Thomas Nelson and Sons, 1965.

WINTER, HERBERT. *Tiffany Favrile Glass*. South Hanover, Massachusetts (1176 Broadway): Privately printed, 1964.

China and Pottery

CUSHION, J. P. *German Ceramic Marks*. London: Faber and Faber, Ltd., 1961. Issued by Boston Book and Art Shop, Boston, Massachusetts, 1962.

JERVIS, W. P. *A Pottery Primer*. New York: The O'Gorman Publishing Company, 1911.

KAMM, MINNIE WATSON. *Old China*. Watkins Glen, New York: Century House Americana, 1951.

KLEIN, WILLIAM KARL. *Repair and Restoration of China and Glass*. Philadelphia (Camac and Grange Streets): Privately printed, 1964.

OWEN, P. *The Story of Bing and Grondahl Danish Christmas Plates*. Dayton, Ohio (1975 Burnham Lane): Viking Import House, 1962.

―――. *The Story of Royal Copenhagen Danish Christmas Plates*. Dayton, Ohio (1975 Burnham Lane): Viking Import House.

RICKERSON, WILDEY G. *Majolica*. Deep River, Connecticut: Privately printed, 1962.

SCHLEIGER, ARLENE. *Two Hundred Patterns of Haviland China, Books I–IV*. Omaha, Nebraska (4039 Mary Street): Privately printed, 1951–1961.

THORN, C. JORDAN. *Handbook of Pottery and Porcelain Marks*. New York: Tudor Publishing Co., 1947.

WARE, GEORGE W. *German and Austrian Porcelain*. New York: Crown Publishers, 1963.

Dolls, Toys, and Games

HART, LOUELLA. *Directory of German Dolls Trademarks, 1875–1960*. Published by author, 1964.

————. *The French Doll Directory, 1801–1964*. Published by author, 1965.

MASORIAK, RAY. *The Curious History of Music Boxes*. Lightner Publishing Company, 1943.

McCLINTOCK, MARSHALL and INEZ. *Toys in America*. Washington: Public Affairs Press, 1961.

ST. GEORGE, ELEANOR. *Old Dolls*. New York: M. Barrows and Company, 1950.

INDEX